Write That Eulogy

The art and craft
of
biographical storytelling

By Veronika Sophia Robinson

Starflower Press

Write That Eulogy: *the art and craft of biographical storytelling*
© Veronika Sophia Robinson
© Cover illustration by Sarah Esau
© Extract from *Changing Places* by Paul Robinson

Published by Starflower Press
ISBN 978-1-7398336-6-4

Cover design, interior design and typesetting: Starflower Press

All rights reserved. No part of this publication may be reproduced, distributed or transmitted in any form or by any means, including photocopying, recording or other electronic or mechanical methods, without the prior written permission of the publisher, except in cases of brief quotations embodied in critical reviews and certain other non-commercial uses permitted by copyright law.

Author's Note: Liberally scattered throughout *Write That Eulogy* are extracts from eulogies I've written. Names and other identifying factors have been changed.

Praise for Write That Eulogy

I found it so incredibly useful to have each stage and writing skill/tool described in such a clear and methodical way. Breaking down the understanding of writing a eulogy, in so many ways, by looking at the areas of life (which I loved!) and also by considering literary elements, made the process of eulogy writing, for me, far less huge and daunting. And that there's no need to sit with a blank piece of paper, wondering where to start. I think my tendency generally is to focus on the 'whole', which turns any task into an enormous monster; I feel I can now tackle a eulogy in stages, in a rather more sensible fashion.

I'm reminded that writing is an on-going process, and the development of skills and, very importantly, attention to the senses, can really make a difference to sensitive and thoughtful writing.

Truly, I loved it; it's accessible, so informative and a joy to read. I also find your ability to share personal information about yourself really heartwarming.
Lorraine Haven, Celebrant, U.K

It provides a step-by-step guide to the multifaceted task of eulogy construction. I think if I was new to the subject, this would be a brilliant guide. Equally, I was riveted, as a more experienced writer. I think all the examples really bring it to life. We never stop learning our trade. It is easy to slip into more mundane ways and this is a beautiful prod to never become boring.

I have learned that there is much technical detail in a eulogy. I think I do lots of it naturally, but it has made me appreciate the complexity of the work. It is written in a way which is accessible to everyone. I'm not sure how you did it, but this book is gold dust to the new, and experienced, alike.
Rachel Cheer, Celebrant, Scotland

This book will definitely help me with eulogy writing. I loved the areas of human life. These will certainly help me to reframe my questioning and help me to get more meaningful information to work with. I also loved reading the scene setting, and again, this made me think about my own style of writing and ways to improve it. This book would be useful for anyone who works with people as it helps you to think 'outside of the box' and question the very essence of human beings.
Lianne Downey, Celebrant, England

Wow! The Twelve Areas of Human Life was absolutely fascinating. Your experience and attention to fact finding and in-depth detail of avoiding the dreaded résumé we so often hear at funerals was not only enlightening but much appreciated.

I have learned so much that I feel my anxiety towards interviewing mourners actually dissolving! Has to be the most interesting "textbook" I've ever had the pleasure of reading.
Kimberlee Brown-Cassady, Celebrant, USA

I loved this book for lots of different reasons. Firstly it was very inviting - it makes you want to be the best you can be at creating a eulogy which honours and tells the story of the deceased.

I loved it, as a newbie to the celebrant world; it's a book that is super insightful, helpful, and packed full of a life's worth of learning to help others be the best they can be at writing that eulogy!
Deborah C. Anderson, Celebrant, England

You make the reader recognise that writing a great eulogy is not for the faint hearted, and you must have a passion for writing and understand the mechanics of it. The anecdotal experiences described give the reader a real sense of the work of a professional celebrant.
Gill Bunting, Celebrant, England

Write That Eulogy has been woven together beautifully; it's an effortless read which can teach an individual a lot about themselves, as well as a craft that you have spent years fine-tuning.
Ben Foreman, Celebrant, Scotland

Dedication

This book is dedicated to two exceptional women:

My mother, Angelikah,
not only for her extraordinary life
and brilliance as a mother
but also because I loved all those afternoons where we
'played' together writing creative fictional sentences.

We had so much fun letting our imaginations
take root and fly.
This is where my love of writing began,
and for this I am indebted.

Tracy Lazonby,
you are so gifted at helping families to arrange
beautiful and personalised funerals.

Thank you for always believing in me,
and trusting me with your families.

The funeral industry isn't an easy one to work in.
Discovering you,
and having the pleasure of working together,
has been (and continues to be) a real joy.
Thank you, thank you, thank you!

Contents

Introduction | 8
Why Have a Eulogy? | 12
Can You Write Your Own Eulogy? | 15
The Curiosity Gene | 18
Fact Gathering | 21
The Areas of Human Life | 26
Your Life is Not a Résumé | 39
Biographical Storytelling | 44
Word Medicine | 47
Literary Elements | 49
Themes and Cinematic Views | 65
Writing Tips | 75
Content and Creative Writing | 112
Difficult Death Stories | 120
Ending the Eulogy | 134
Remembering | 147
Editing the Eulogy | 155
Other Tips |156
Show The Script | 160
From Writing to Officiating | 163
What Have You Learned? | 164

Introduction

For many years, I'd worked as a celebrant officiating across all rites of passage, except funerals. I'd created private memorials for women to honour and mourn miscarriages and termination, but there was no way I was going to lead a public funeral service. Not a chance! It was an impossible task. Why? Because, as an empath, I knew I couldn't stand in front of a congregation of mourners and not end up crying. And so, for years and years I avoided it. Until the time I was dragged, kicking and screaming, to the lectern at a crematorium. (Okay, kicking, perhaps, but not screaming). To be fair, I did have five years to prepare for the funeral. I knew it was on the cards. I'd previously served the family in question as a wedding celebrant and as a naming celebrant. As far as they were concerned, no one else could possibly be the celebrant. How could I say no?

I don't know if I ever prayed as hard as I did the day I got the phone call that Colin had died. I begged whoever was listening, somewhere amongst the energies of the Universe, to help me through my fear. And so the day finally came: and to a packed, standing-room-only crematorium, I led mourners in ceremony. We remembered a man who'd been well-known and popular in his community, and was dearly loved. As I stepped out of the crematorium after the ceremony, one by one people came to me and said it was the most beautiful funeral they'd ever

been to. I was struck by this comment. If that was the most beautiful funeral they'd ever been to, what on Earth was happening at other funerals? I've since learned, having heard those comments repeatedly over the years, that there are three things which shine from my services:
1. My authenticity and genuine care
2. My writing and storytelling style
3. And that I don't read off a résumé

I recently officiated a funeral for a man who'd requested me after seeing me officiate his son's wedding some five years earlier. His ceremony was a pleasure to write as he'd left copious and descriptive notes about his wonderful life. A woman came to me afterwards and said she'd been to five funerals in the past fortnight and that four of them were boring and/or terrible, and this one had been brilliant. It's not unusual for me to hear from mourners that they'd really "enjoyed" a ceremony. Sometimes they feel guilty for saying it, as if there's something fundamentally wrong with finding pleasure in a funeral.

Write That Eulogy was written to bring a transformation to the tired traditional telling of eulogies. To be clear, this book hasn't been written specifically for celebrants, but for anyone who is considering writing their life story, or someone else's, so it is told faithfully at their funeral. If you are willing to question what's always been done, then you're half way there to improving funeral ceremonies.

My second reason for penning *Write That Eulogy* is because of the times of immense frustration when visiting some families. I go there, hopeful to learn of their loved one, only to have each question answered with "I don't know". While it's fair to say that grief can close us down, and make it hard to remember, sometimes it's just a matter of a lack of curiosity. I've often wondered how can you be married to someone for forty years and not know anything about them. How is it that humans can pay so little attention to others? What happened to curiosity? It's disheartening to me, when I'm relying on loved ones to share memories, for them to have so little recollection.

I love to know about other people. And this genuine interest and curiosity shines through in my celebrant work. One of my skills is to be able to write a meaningful and personalised eulogy regardless of how scant the information I have to work with (even though it can be frustrating). The more stories and facts which are shared, the better.

The benefit of writing your own eulogy is that YOU (and you alone) know everything about your life. You can also choose what you'd like to share with others, and that which you wish to leave behind.

I've learnt many things since I began work as a funeral celebrant, such as mastering emotions, and how to step into another's shoes and tell their story with respect, creativity and flair.

In this book you can expect to find my best tips, extracts from eulogies, ways to craft your story or someone else's, and ideas on how to ensure the whole ceremony reflects the person you're writing about. Whether you work as a celebrant, are a celebrant-in-training, or have chosen to write a eulogy for a loved one or yourself, I trust you'll find this book inspiring. Enjoy.

Crafting a eulogy in praise of someone's life is akin to pressing beautiful flowers between the pages of a book.

It's our way of holding onto a little of what we cherished, so we can keep them close just that bit longer.

Why Have a Eulogy?

The word eulogy comes from the Greek, and means 'to bless' or 'true words of praise'. The eulogy has become synonymous with a funeral ceremony. It is optional, though. At its most basic level, the purpose of a funeral is to legally and hygienically 'dispose' of a dead body. Some people choose the option of either a direct cremation or direct burial. It's become increasingly common for two reasons:

1. to cut down on funeral costs and avoid funeral poverty
2. To avoid fuss.

In many cases, even when a direct cremation/burial has been chosen, there often comes a time when loved ones choose a memorial service. Why? *Because the human soul craves a sense of the sacred.* There's a need to honour, reflect, remember; to hold a loved one's memories in reverence, and to bid farewell with grace and compassion.

At the heart of any funeral ceremony is the liminal (transitional/threshold) space we enter into. And it is here that I, as a funeral celebrant, offer the story of a person's life.

Recently, I came out of the crematorium after officiating a funeral ceremony, and a woman came up to me and said "I was (deceased's name) best friend for forty years, and I didn't know half the stuff you shared today." To me, that's the sign of a great eulogy: we learn more about the person we knew.

One gentleman came up to me after a ceremony and asked if I'd written the service. I thought it an odd question.
"Yes," I replied.
"But did you write *all* of it?"
"Yes," I repeated.
He then continued. "I've been writing eulogies all of my adult life," he said (turns out he was a vicar), "and I've never heard a eulogy like that. I've worked with (name) for years and years. You've just painted this panoramic view of her whole life. I feel like I really know her now."

Another woman came to me after a ceremony, touched me gently on the arm, and said her mother had died during the pandemic and how horrendous the funeral experience had been. "This ceremony was deeply healing for me. Thank you."

One thing I hear repeatedly from the families I am privileged to serve is how I've truly captured the essence of their loved one. They're perplexed as to how I did that when I've never met them. The key is in the listening. Not just the words a family may say, but what they *don't* say. I watch for body language, too. So much can be heard in the silence.

Depending on the venue chosen for the ceremony, I'm often under a tight time frame. It's a constant source of stress as a celebrant if you work primarily out of a crematorium with short slots. For example, the main crematorium I work at has a forty-minute slot (that is, there is a service *every* forty minutes). Many families think it means they get a forty-minute ceremony. The reality is a twenty-minute ceremony. The other twenty minutes are to get people into and out of the chapel. The greeting line after a ceremony can take a long time. So depending on music choices, readings, additional tributes, and allowing for words of welcome, the committal, a prayer, and closing words, I have about *four to eight minutes* to sum up a person's life. It's a balance between enormously frustrating and deeply rewarding. It takes skill, creativity, care and awareness of the human story.

(During the tightest restrictions of the pandemic, when we had to be in and out of the crematorium in 15 minutes, it was so stressful. Mourners had to be seated two metres apart, even if they lived together. Hugging [my main currency!] was strictly forbidden. Mourner numbers were limited to just eight. It's no wonder so many families were traumatised. And can you imagine if you're from a large family and having to decide who could and couldn't go to the ceremony?)

Can You Write Your Own Eulogy?

Yes, you can write your own eulogy, and there are many reasons why you should.

When I'm training new celebrants, I often suggest that they take some time to write their own eulogy. Why? Because, as Joseph Campbell once said, "Every story we tell is our own story." By examining our own life, and reflecting on what is meaningful to us, we'll have a deeper insight into how to share other people's stories. It's not a measure of ego to write your own eulogy any more than it is to write an autobiography. It is the sharing of our lifestory from our own perspective.

Amongst my favourite eulogies are those I've written for people I spoke to while they were alive. There are certain challenges in conversing with someone on their deathbed as they go in and out consciousness, but the honesty and direct sharing of information leads to a completely different storytelling.

I've had my fair share of situations where those who were left with the task of organising a funeral simply had no interest in the deceased. I've heard words such as "I hated her" or "We don't even want a funeral for him!" And with heavy heart, I weed through their anger, regret, jealousy, frustration or contempt to find the essence of a person who can no longer speak for themselves.

Death and funerals bring out people's true colours: the best and the worst of the human personality. I remember being with one family where each person only had negative things to say about the deceased. My job is made infinitely harder in these situations.

Here are two reasons to write your own eulogy:
1. You tell your story. This means that what was important to you, and what you found meaningful, will shine through in your ceremony. You're not reliant on someone else's memory, and you certainly don't have to have your life story told by those who didn't like you or weren't that interested in you.
2. It's a gift to your loved ones. In the UK, a chief mourner has between 80 to 300 decisions to make after their loved one dies. It could be decisions to do with the funeral, such as cremation or burial, or sandwiches or sausage rolls at the funeral tea. There's a lot of work involved in tidying up 'loose ends', whether it's financial, legal or otherwise. Having your story written (whether in the form of notes, or in the first person, third person or as a collection of tributes) makes so much difference. It's as if a real weight comes off the shoulders of family members.

There'll be decisions to make such as where your funeral is likely to be. This will determine the length of the eulogy. For example, if the whole ceremony is graveside you're unlikely to have a half-hour service (unless there is seating in place or great weather).

I've officiated my share of ceremonies in sub-zero temperatures, gale-force winds and torrential rain. All the work that's gone into writing a beautiful ceremony can easily be lost in fifty-mile-per-hour winds. In a crematorium, there are time restrictions. A ceremony in a different venue (e.g. home, garden, hotel, village hall) gives a sense of freedom, and might be the ideal place for your goodbye.

If I can see pain in your eyes,
then share with me your tears.

If I can see joy in your eyes,
then share with me your smile.
~ Santosh Kalwar

The Curiosity Gene

If you're a celebrant or an officiant, your business is to create. As human beings, we are designed to create. Creativity begins with curiosity.

In my early twenties, I approached the editor of my local newspaper with a view to getting some work as a reporter. As I sat at Neil's desk (a man I'll always be grateful to for giving me my start in journalism), he asked me what the clouds looked like as I drove to the newspaper office that afternoon.

What? The clouds? What a ridiculous question! Turns out, it wasn't so ridiculous. His question changed my life. What he wanted to find out was how observant I was. I might have failed that test, but he certainly discovered that my curiosity was not in short supply. Neil took me on, inviting me to come into the editorial room each afternoon after my day job, and do the emergency rounds. My role was to phone the fire, ambulance and police stations, and see if there were any stories to follow up.

By the Friday of that first week, Neil said "I don't have a reporter available for this weekend's stories. Can you do it?"

"Hell yeah!" (My usual answer to any adventure or opportunity!)

Right then and there he passed me a Ricoh camera, showed me how to load a black-and-white film, and gave me a list of the jobs. By Monday morning, I had my first front-page story! And before long, I had my first feature article: the life story of a local radiographer, Wally, who'd been the second person ever to have had penicillin.

Sometimes, when the film was developed, Neil would say "How did you get this photo?"
"Oh I hitched a ride on a boat to the middle of the lake" or "I climbed a ladder!"

Neil would pull his hair out and say "Our insurance doesn't cover that! Keep both feet on dry earth!" I might have infuriated him, but he secretly loved my curiosity and ability to see things from a different view.

Curiosity can also lead to truth. How can I ever forget that Christmas Eve when I was five and went to spy on Santa only to discover it was my father who put the presents under the tree?

The depth and breadth of your creativity is in direct proportion to your curiosity.

One reason travelling is an expansive way of living is that the traveller's mind sees things in a new way. Although we consider sight to be a visual perception, when we see something, 80% of it is to do with *memory*, and only 20% to do with our eyes. Sensory information comes *from* the brain, not to it.

Curiosity Killed The Cat
Write a few paragraphs about something you did in childhood that involved curiosity (for better or worse). Write it in the first person, then again in the third person.

The depth and breadth of your creativity is in direct proportion to your curiosity.

Fact Gathering

I've never gone into a family meeting with prepared questions. Instead, I gently walk into the memories they hold of the deceased's life. I avoid 'yes/no' questions, and never say "So, what can you tell me about Fred?" This type of question, for most mourners, is meaningless. They need guidance, direction and encouragement to enter their memory pathways. Take their metaphorical hand, and lead the way; ask questions that will soon have them racing down forgotten lanes.

My questions might look like this: "I see there are recipe books on the shelf. What did Adelaide like to cook?" "Who did she cook for?" "What was her favourite recipe?" "How and where did she learn to cook?" One question should have the potential to lead to several other questions.

So I might come home with notes like this:
Veronika Robinson, born in Brisbane, Australia. Lived in the UK for…years. At the age of five, chose to become vegetarian. Her dad then bought land to raise beef cattle. As an adult, she wrote two vegan cookery books. Loved cooking for others, and appreciated the sensual nature of good food.

Raised on 700 acres on the Darling Downs in South-East Queensland from the age of six. Amazing childhood, with mountains, creeks, dams, fields and hills. One of eight children. Often played on her own as she liked solitude. Always up a tree. Her dad worked overseas, in Papua and New Guinea, away from home for several weeks at a time. Amazing mother who was the ultimate earth mother and chose natural alternative therapies such as colour healing.

V remembers many nights sleeping on the trampoline with her mum, and her joy of the unpolluted night skies, and how the southern hemisphere stars are etched in her memory. Said she never could learn the northern hemisphere constellations.

Raised on a horsestud, and lived her childhood on the back of a horse. Excellent horse rider. No longer rides due to old injuries. Strong memories include: a bunch of the kids inside an old corrugated-iron rainwater tank, tipped on its side, and rolling along the road in it completely blind to any potential traffic on the dusty dirt road.

Power of her mind. Aged about 8, V stood on a rusty nail and developed blood poisoning. Her mother pointed to the red line going up her leg and explained that if it reached her heart, she'd die. She had to imagine that line going back down to her foot and disappearing. Her mum sat her on the outside steps, placed her foot in a bowl of Dettol water, and left her to it.

Another life-changing experience was firewalking (aged 19 and 21), and realising the power of the mind. It remained a highlight of her life.

And so my notes continue. My job is to 'make magic', and to take these facts, as told to me, and create a coherent story.

When taking notes, I don't rely on my (fantastic) memory but write down every single thing I hear, and always double-check spelling or that I've understood something correctly. It's not unusual for me to have to write about something unfamiliar to me: bomb disposal, abattoir, a shooting range, and so on. This was also my experience, many years ago, when working as a journalist. I was often exposed to things completely out of my life experience or frame of reference. The key is to keep asking questions, and never be afraid to look ignorant. I try to avoid having to come back to my mourners to ask questions. My job is to gather all my information, where possible, during my visit.

Some notes from my meeting about Cassandra
Lived in the village her whole life (born in the house she lived in).
Mum and grandmother grew herbs and sold their products.
Everyone bought her products even if they didn't admit it.
No children of her own, but all the children in the village loved her and would regularly visit for a cup of tea (and the hope of having their tea leaves read).
Kettle always on Aga.
Her wisdom was legendary.
Always giving people plants from her herb garden.
Well-known for gardening by and under the Moon.
If anyone in the village was ever ill, she'd leave a

concoction on their doorstep with instructions on how to use it. Even the local GP would send patients to her. People often wondered if she might be lonely (no husband/kids) but nobody can recall a time of her not smiling.

My First Draft

Nobody quite remembers the village without a medicine woman, yet they all agree that Cassandra was a third-generation herbalist who learnt at the feet of her maternal grandmother. Older denizens remember how she never left Granny Nell's side, until the day the old woman died, and was often scribbling words and sketching botanical illustrations in an old notebook.

Dried herbs hung from every hook in the ceiling, tied with raffia, or bunched in Hessian bags. Rows and rows of balms, tinctures, lotions and potions lined the pine Irish dressers, and filled every corner of the pantry. With her calligraphy-style handwriting, each label was almost a piece of art. Sometimes people wondered if her favourite colour was dark blue as that was the only coloured bottle she'd store her products in.

It was well known that if you happened to wander by Sage Cottage under the light of the Full Moon, Cassandra would be in her garden, barefoot, humming an Old Polish tune. And with a basket in her hand, she harvested herbs. These simple plants changed people's lives. Fevers eased. Broken bones knitted back together. Appetite returned. Fragile pregnancies made it to full term. A miracle worker, they called her.

Cassandra never minded the sceptics and anyone else who scoffed at her work, because she knew, that at some point, they'd turn up at her door determined to get to the bottom of an ailment. Even the local doctor directed patients her way.

The kettle rested on top of the Aga, only ever a few minutes away from topping up a tea pot. Every single child within a three-mile radius would sneak to her cottage in the hope of having their tea leaves read. More than anything, though, they came because of her kindness: the extra lavender cookies she'd slip into their pockets, or a few pennies to help their mother pay a vet bill or buy groceries; and how she'd sometimes help them with their homework.

We learn quite a lot about Cassandra in these few paragraphs: her ancestry, her home, her work, her place in the community, and her kindness.

The Areas of Human Life

What questions do you ask a mourner? How do you know what's important? These are questions often asked of me by celebrants-in-training. Although I don't go in with a list of questions, I do carry *within* me an awareness of the areas of human life. To be clear, I don't necessarily ask questions or lead conversation into all these areas, but I do draw upon them if I feel the family needs some help to explore memories.

This chapter serves the purpose of expanding how you view 'the human story'. As an illustration, I've included some 'fact gathering' examples from my own life.

Thinking about these areas will allow you to be more creative in your conversations with mourners. Start by exploring your own life, then those nearest and dearest to you. It will soon become second nature to see other's lives through the lens of the twelve areas.

I want to be all used up when I die.
~ George Bernard Shaw

The First Area: *The Physical Self*

This part of human life covers things like physical appearance, how we move or present ourselves to the world. It might show up as mannerisms or whether we are shy and reserved, or gregarious, vivacious. It's both physical and energetic.

Perhaps we're physically beautiful or maybe we have a physical limitation. You can think of this area as like the 'front door' to who we are. It's one aspect of us, but most certainly not all of us. Maybe we have scoliosis (curvature of the spine), eczema (skin itches all the time). Perhaps we have an athlete's body.

Fact gathering: 5.7 tall, top heavy, green eyes (only 2% of the population has green eyes), good skin, strong bones. Inherited my dad's flat bum, hollow chest, and my mum's Germanic cheekbones and eyes. I'm a sociable introvert. As a young child (before we moved to the countryside), I loved to stand at the front of the garden and say hello to any stranger who walked by. I'm always talking to strangers in the supermarket, and love to compliment people on their clothes, etc.

Can You Recognise Me?
Describe your physical appearance. If you were meeting a stranger somewhere, how could they identify you (without necessarily mentioning clothing)? Silver hair? Tall? Red cheeks? A limp? Think about mannerisms, and body language.

The Second Area: *Values*

In this area of life, we explore our values and sense of worth. What is important to us? What do we treasure? Money in the bank? A pantry full of food? Jewellery? Land or home ownership?

Fact gathering: I value books (knowledge), beauty (environment, colour, especially flowers) and music. Love having bowls of fresh fruit and flowers in my home. I value discipline, dedication, and organisational skills. My top three values: beauty, integrity, simplicity.

The Treasure Chest

In childhood, we soon learn what is valuable to us: a teddy, Matchbox car, cuddles, friendships, books, tree climbing.

What are your values, and what do you value? (They're two different things)

How might these show in a eulogy about your life? Write a few paragraphs, in the third person, exploring these. In essence, this about the things/experiences in your treasure chest.

The Third Area: *Communication*

In this area we look at aspects of communication: speaking, writing, teaching, learning; and how we interact in our local neighbourhood. How about early schooling and siblings? These could come into this area, after all, in our formative years we learn so much about how to express ourselves through those around us. Maybe it's about working out cryptic crosswords or playing Scrabble. How about a quick-sense of humour? In short, this area is about how we connect with others and the world through our writing, speaking and learning.

Fact gathering: I am one of eight children (five brothers, two sisters), and I'm slap bang in the middle of them. I hated school with a passion, and spent more time wagging (playing truant) than in the classroom. I'd often head down to the Condamine River and go swimming. In my life I've been a teacher (of children and adults); in Montessori and Steiner Schools; Riding for the Disabled; a trainer; and a workshop facilitator. I've worked as a journalist on local, regional and city newspapers as well as a media officer. Love humour, and laughing till my sides ache.

Every Day Is a Learning Day
Reflect on your early schooling (not so much about where, unless there's something interesting about it), but your *experience* of it. Also, consider your communication style (perhaps as seen through someone else's eyes).

The Fourth Area: *Where Do I Come From?*

This isn't so much about a bricks-and-mortar home (though it absolutely can be), but more about what makes us 'feel at home'. Maybe home was a bohemian affair with bright colours and people from all walks of life coming and going, philosophers, travellers: a real open home. We could have felt most alive by all this energy or violated by the lack of privacy. Maybe home was behind a security gate, with only the rare few stepping over the threshold. Could it be that home/ancestry is shrouded in mystery? A secret adoption? Where do we come from? Home is also where we psychologically undress from the world.

Fact gathering: Our 300-year-old cottage has a high hedge at one side, a field with grazing sheep on another, apple trees, raspberries and blueberries in the garden, and a high stone wall on the other. This privacy is perfect for me. It's a place held up by books; with two affectionate cats; and generally with something delicious simmering on the stovetop. Music playing and incense burning will let you know I'm home. The main home of my childhood was a remote horse stud in rural Australia.

Home Sweet Home. Or Is It?
Think about home, and also what makes you *feel* at home. Explore what this means to you, both in terms of the home you live in now, and where you were raised. Try writing a few paragraphs.

The Fifth Area: *Creativity & Risk Taking*

This area covers all manner of things. In one sense, it could be considered to be about risk taking. That includes gambling, creativity, love affairs and having children. In short, it is about how we express ourself. It's also about how we experience fun and pleasure. For one person, this might mean curling up on the sofa reading a romance novel. And for another, it could be their Thursday-night salsa class or learning to draw.

Fact gathering: Mother of two daughters. Creativity as a writer and celebrant. Once worked as a recreational therapist in an Alzheimer's care home. I've also been white-water rafting in New Zealand, and swimming with dolphins in the open ocean. I have the National Lotto app on my phone, and believe that 'you've got to be in it to win it!'. I love to cook!

Play Time
Think about the life of someone you know well, and how these various aspects show up in their life. What is their expression of play, fun, creativity and risk taking. Write three paragraphs.

Explore why being creative is an act of risk taking.

The Sixth Area: *Work and Health*

Our day-to-day lives are intimately woven with the stories of our work and wellbeing. This area can include domestic pets, habits, health, alternative health, and our work colleagues. There's a distinct connection between mind, body and soul. This area is to do with our daily rhythm.

Fact gathering: I rarely go to doctors (I've never had a positive experience with them), and prefer natural immunity and alternative therapies: reflexology, acupuncture, etc. Two cats: Pele and Kali (had cats most of my life). My daily practices: plant-based diet, barefoot on the grass, abdominal and nasal breathing, meditating, gratitude.

Find Your Rhythm
Describe your daily rhythm both in terms of health/illness, self-care practices, day-to-day work and rituals, and any mind-body-soul approaches.

Write a few paragraphs (in third person) and then try doing the same for someone in your life.

The Seventh Area: *The Intimate Other*

In this area, we look to our intimate relationships. This could be one like marriage, a business partnership or even that of a mentor or counsellor.

Fact gathering: My husband and I met in 1995, and he moved in the day after he came over for dinner.

We combine our skills in a shared business (as celebrant trainers working one-to-one with those in training). I've worked as a mentor and psychological astrologer, and enjoy the one-to-one relationships.

Who Am I When I Am With You?
Think about the one-to-one relationships in your life. What do these look like? Are they personal or professional? The theme of this area is partnership. That is: *Who am I when I'm with you?*

Write two paragraphs exploring this both from first-person and third-person points of view.

Consider how different parts of your personality are expressed depending on who you are around.

The Eighth Area: *Transformation*

In this part, we look at areas of transformation: birth, death, sex, other people's money (shared resources) e.g. inheritance, debt, taxes; psychology. It might show up in someone who works as a debt collector or banker, or a funeral arranger or a midwife, for example.

Please note: I'm absolutely NOT suggesting you ask a mourner about the deceased's sex life! I'm only including it here because it's an area of transformation. It's where we 'surrender' ourselves to another (for better or worse). Of course, that's not to say you might never write a eulogy for someone who works in this field. E.g. sexually-transmitted-infections counsellor or sexuality psychologist or rape counsellor.

Fact gathering: I set up the National Waterbirth Trust in New Zealand; wrote a book about natural birth; and am passionate about home birth. I work as a funeral celebrant entering the world of other people's grief. As a self-employed person, having to do my annual accounts each year is a pain in the …

Changing Doors
How have you been changed by the experiences listed in the area of transformation?

Write two to three paragraphs, in the third person, exploring this.

The Ninth Area: *Beyond the Horizon*

The desire to 'see the beyond the horizon' is particularly strong for some people. In this area, we would explore topics like university education (higher learning) either as a student or a lecturer/professor, foreign travel, foreign culture, foreign languages, publishing, and even horses, and wide open spaces. A sport like archery would fit into this area (the arrow searching for a point in the distance).

Fact gathering: I was raised on a horse stud on seven hundred acres in rural Australia. My parents were German immigrants. At the age of 22, I applied to be an air hostess (and passed through three interview stages). I moved to New Zealand at aged 23. I've travelled to many countries (and have moved countries six times). I've published magazines and books (three of which have been translated into other languages), and earned a Master's degree through the University of Cumbria.

Beyond The Horizon
What themes from area nine can you see in your own life? How might you write about them? Is there anyone in your family or friendship circle who shares similar experiences? If so, write three paragraphs about them.

The Tenth Area: *Where We Shine*

This area may be expressed in a highly visible career, or in the ways you shine out in the world. You may have won awards, for example. Perhaps you've been on TV or in the press?

Fact gathering: I'm not famous, yet much of my work has been out in public (public speaking, books being read around the world, media appearances).

> *Grief is the price we pay for love.*
> ~ Queen Elizabeth II

Your Name in Lights
Consider where you 'shine' in the world. Have you won awards? Is your work in the public eye in some way? In what part of your life are you most visible to others? This area of career is different to area six (day-to-day work). The latter would include more mundane jobs.

The Eleventh Area: *Our Humanitarian Self*

These are the topics I'd explore in this area: Community, friendships, humanity. It's about how we connect to others in the world (but in a different way to, say, the more intimate nature of having a best friend or a spouse).

Fact Gathering: I see this in the volunteer work I've done in my lifetime: teaching Riding for Disabled; reading books to people in a hospice; visiting people in care homes; delivering Meals on Wheels; and as a celebrant officiating wedding ceremonies where a person is terminally ill. Donating to charities: Action Aid, Water Aid, Trussell Trust (food banks); Tree Sisters.

Great Big Melting Pot
Write down four examples of humanitarianism from your own life, and that of someone else you know. Then, write a few paragraphs about this in the third person as if it were being shared in a eulogy.

The Twelfth Area: *Behind Closed Doors*

This is about the less-visible parts of human existence; what I like to think of as 'behind closed doors'. It could, for example, be someone who has spent a lot of time in hospital (professionally or as a patient), in jail (professionally or as an inmate), in a monastery or a convent. It can also cover spirituality (as opposed to religion). It may include someone who has a deep appreciation of solitude or likes to live or work on their own away from the eyes of others. Often this features strongly in the life of writers, artists and composers who spend most of their time in an imaginal world. Spiritual practices such as meditation or prayer would fit into this area.

Fact gathering: I've worked in a hospital. I consider myself to be deeply spiritual. Solitude is my sanctuary. Amongst my greatest joys are immersing myself in spiritual learnings. My first talk at school was on reincarnation.

Invisible World
What parts of your life feel like they're lived behind closed doors? Explore this in a few paragraphs, told in the third person.

Your Life is Not a Résumé

Traditionally, eulogies have been written in chronological order as if our lives are to be read as a résumé. Although it is true that we live our lives from one day to the next, from one age to the next, until our allotted chapters are completed, our life story certainly doesn't need to be told in that order, and nor does it need to be a bland statement of facts.

> *Erini de Rosa was born on the 21st August, 1973. Her father was a lion tamer, and her mother was a trapeze artist. Erini lived with the (name of) Circus until she was 15.*

OR

> *There were two things Erini learnt from being a lion tamer's daughter: lion saliva has antiseptic qualities; taming is an illusion. When Claude Bottom (her father's stage name), was mauled to death by his favourite lion, Erini ran away from the circus.*

Consider these two openings:

> *Dagmar Hellwig was born in Germany on 27th May, 1939. The war years meant living off meagre rations of food. Some of her siblings died in infancy, and she hated death.*

OR

> *Ich liebe dich*
> *Te Amo*
> *Jag älskar dig*
> *Rakastan sinua*
> *Mi lavim yu*
>
> *Dagmar could say I love you in several languages. A romantic at heart, she wove her way through this world by ensuring she spread love and beauty wherever she passed.*

How do you feel about the differences in style between traditional eulogy writing and creative storytelling?

> *Miranda Blackwell was born on March 20th, 1950, the fourth child of Mary and Martin. Martin was stationed in (name of place). His job with (name of charity) meant he was in charge of 50 volunteers who were installing wells and building other services.*
>
> *The family lived there for five years. Miranda was home tutored by her mother, a former teacher. Mary was killed by travelling bandits searching their home for jewellery and other valuables. Upon their return to (town), Martin's mental health deteriorated and he was unable to work. Miranda went to live with her grandmother for the rest of her childhood.*

OR

Every Sunday morning, Miranda lay in bed until the church bells rang. Within seconds, she'd be showered, dressed and had switched on the stereo. At full volume, she'd listen to Puccini while preparing the Sunday lunch. Married to a vicar, it fell upon her to entertain parishioners. Having learnt to cook from her grandmother, it was something which came easily to her. Whether she cooked for four or forty, it always brought her joy.

What she wouldn't do, what she never *did, was go to church. Miranda promised Vince, the day they married (not in his church but in the registry office) that she'd make it 'worth his while'. And she most certainly did. From dancing in St Mark's Square in Venice to trekking Kilimanjaro to sailing in the Bahamas to riding elephants in Sri Lanka, they created a lifetime of memories. Their relationship was dynamic, fun, interesting, and in Vince's words, deeply passionate, but what they didn't share in common was a love of the Divine. Miranda said "If God exists, he's the enemy." Vince hadn't walked in Miranda's shoes, but as a man of empathy he understood how she'd come to that decision. Right from day one, he never sought to answer the one question that always remained on Miranda's lips: "Why was my mother killed?"*

I imagine that when someone walks out at the end of one of my funeral ceremonies, they can't quite put their finger on why it was different to other funerals they've been to. It's because: *the human life is not a résumé.* And it is for this reason that I don't write eulogies in that way.

Rarely do I use dates, and probably only one in 100 of my funerals is written in anywhere near chronological order. This one distinct difference does two things:

1. Allows for creative flair and brings the deceased 'to life' for the duration of the memory sharing
2. Focuses on showing who the deceased was rather than telling the audience.

Keep love in your heart.
A life without it is like a sunless garden
when the flowers are dead.
~ Oscar Wilde

Jack Smith was born on June 1st, 1924. He was raised in Manchester by Sue and Phillip Smith. They had four sons who all went to the local grammar school.

I honestly want to tear my hair out when I hear and read eulogies like this. Why? Because I don't learn who the person was. When I write a eulogy, I do so with the idea that a complete stranger might be amongst the mourners. I want them to come away feeling like they'd known the deceased. If they feel like that, then my chief mourner will feel I have captured their loved one's essence too.

People will rarely remember the dates spoken in a eulogy unless the date was significant to them in some way. I certainly use time signatures (more on that later) but in a different way than stating a date.

If you want to breathe life into your writing, follow me.

Biographical Storytelling

Another way that my approach to celebrancy differs from many funeral celebrants is that I don't go into a mourner's home with a list of questions. This industry attracts a lot of retired police officers and murder detectives. Over and over I've heard them say that celebrancy is no different. "You just go in with a bunch of questions!"

Not this celebrant. Yes, there are a few questions I would routinely ask: *What music would you like? Do you want the curtains closed after the committal? Will there be donations? Is there a funeral tea afterwards?* Other than those questions, the rest of my time with a family/mourner is completely organic. Anything that's important to my mourner will come up at some time in our chatting. First and foremost, I want the person/people I'm with to feel 100% comfortable with me, and to feel free to share information about their loved one. This is one of the few jobs where you have to develop trust as quickly as possible.

I naturally begin the conversation in as relaxed a way as possible. It might be a comment about a piece of furniture in their home, or photos on the wall, or about a pet. Once we're in our seats, the conversation is likely to continue in the same relaxed way without the mourner realising I'm 'gathering' information the whole time. What I don't do (and what I train celebrants to avoid) is asking something like "Tell me about Jack." This is unlikely to bring forth anything significant with the majority of mourners. They need guidance. That's the reason I avoid questions which have 'yes' or 'no' answers. The key to good questioning is to ask things which will encourage loved ones to speak and to be keen to share stories.

First and foremost I want to discover the essence of who the person was in life. I want to leave that meeting feeling as if I'd known the person (and that I wished I'd known them). Now, in cases where someone has been ill for a long time or suffered with a debilitating illness like Alzheimer's, it can be all but impossible for families to remember a time when their loved one was younger, healthier, vibrant and passionate about life. My job is to guide them back there.

First and foremost, I like to learn about what brought meaning to a person's days, and the pleasures which filled their life. Even when the person's career was everything, I tend to devote at least half of the eulogy to other parts of their life.

As an information gatherer, I write down everything I hear. Now, sometimes, because of the trust I've built with my family, they'll share things with me that they don't want said in public. In those cases, I put my pen down and simply listen. They have my assurance that there won't be anything said that they haven't approved. All my clients get a copy of the script within about 24 to 48 hours of my visit. This gives them time to let me know if they'd like any amendments. Occasionally, clients will see in black and white what they've said, and realise they either remembered something wrongly or exaggerated. Conscious that people will be listening to the story, they decide to 'change' their recollection to make it more palatable to Aunty Mildred. As I always say, "You only get one chance at this ceremony, so it has to be right!"

I learn as much from what isn't said, and from body language, as I do from the stories I'm told.

After all, what's a life, anyway?
We're born, we live a little while, we die.
~ E.B. White

Word Medicine

First and foremost, I see my writing as word medicine. Medicine (whether allopathic or alternative) is designed to aid the healing process. How might my words heal? How might your words heal?

I also see words as containers: they hold power. Have you considered the words you write as containers? They are, indeed, vessels which allow you to paint pictures onto the page. You have the opportunity to offer healing to those who'll hear your ceremony.

Crafting a script is an art. Each word must enliven the script, tell the story, and be a doorkeeper to feelings. Words are chosen for memory, guidance, instruction, hope, humour, brevity, clarity, flair, beauty, inspiration, entertainment, and healing.

When choosing a word, consider it as a container: what does it hold? Is it the right word? Is there a better word? Maybe it's an unnecessary word that needs ditching and surgically removing in the editing process? Let your words come alive in you. Give them room to breathe. If they don't hold resonance, let them scamper off like giggling children. Strong, powerful words are your ballast, and yet even they can make room for a climbing rose.

Consider how each word feels within your body? How does it sound to your ear? Do you feel it in your heart? Have you read it out loud to understand how it will sound from your mouth? Where else in your body do you *feel* the word? These questions are crucial, and also highlight why you should always write your own scripts rather than have a ghost-celebrant write them.

We never know when or how someone will be changed by our work. Medicine is given in careful doses. A prescription is timed with this in mind, for even with a spoonful of sugar the contents are not meant to be glugged. And may it be so with our words: Careful. Conscious. Clear.

May our vessels offer succour, solace and serenity in challenging times.

Each day I remind myself that I'm a doorkeeper to people's feelings, and with each drop of illumined ink on the page I work to paint pictures.

Literary Elements

So you've spent a couple of hours with a family or chief mourner, and have pages and pages of notes. Or perhaps you're writing your own eulogy. What do you do with all this information? How do you put this into something that's coherent and eloquent? While it's true that there are celebrants who simply read out the information they've written down without crafting, as such, if you wish to write something memorable, you've got a lot of (rewarding) work ahead of you.

First and foremost, you have to think like a *writer* and take your craft seriously. Regardless of whether we write fiction or non-fiction, our job is to offer a lens through which the reader/listener enters another world. The lens is more attractive when it is an emotional one. This can only be built on research, accuracy and perspective. Many people who embark on writing a eulogy feel that there isn't room for creativity because it has to be factual and realistic. By the time you've finished reading *Write That Eulogy* you'll understand that it can be both factual and creative.

Although my use of literary elements in eulogy writing is instinctive (that is, I don't think about it, it happens naturally), let me break it down so you can understand how they bring biographical storytelling alive.

Key literary elements include:
1. Scene setting
2. Character
3. Imagery
4. Point of view
5. Dialogue (monologue)

As a novelist, my books might be based on either character or plot. As a non-fiction writer of eulogies, my storytelling is based on character. With this in mind, let's look at the literary elements to see how they can support this.

Scene Setting
Why might a sense of place be important in showing the character of the person?

The following paragraph from one of my eulogies sets the scene:

> *Born within earshot of Bow Bells, the famous bells of St Mary le Bow, in what is now known as London's East End, Max Allonby arrived into this world destined to be an only child. Cockney by birth and character, a strong work ethic would lead him his whole long life. Despite the absence of siblings, Max was surrounded by children. It was wartime, and ragamuffin kids played in the street, rummaging on hands and knees through rubble, scouring their impromptu playground for shrapnel to play with. They formed friendly little street gangs, and lived their tender lives beneath the loud,*

rattling noise of the doodlebugs. At night, Max would head home to his mum, a hardworking woman who, although she wasn't a single mother, in reality that's what her life was like.

What do we learn about Max from this paragraph?
.He's an only child.
.He grew up in the war.
.Like most children, he was adaptable; and, despite the war, he still had fun and some of the normal things of childhood: play and friendships.

I could have just written: *Max grew up in wartime.* Would that have been enough to take you into his childhood?

Scene setting gives us an emotional viewfinder in which to enter a person's life. It also offers us an opportunity to learn about a person's character. Who they are, and what they look like or their mannerisms, are quite different from each other, yet both contribute to painting a picture. If we think of our eulogy writing from an image-based or senses-based perspective, we develop storytelling skills which take us light years away from traditional eulogy writing.

The point of view of a eulogy is, in most cases, written in the third person. That is, if I'm the celebrant, I'm speaking on behalf of the family. Now it is possible that the eulogy has been written in the first person by the deceased before they passed and you're presenting it in that format. Other points of view include the reminiscences of others. More on that later.

Another way I do this is through dialogue. Dialogue can work in two ways: it could be that you're quoting something the deceased used to say (certain expressions) or you could be quoting someone's thoughts about the deceased.

> *Janice, her best friend, said "Sally was so easy to love."*

Quite often, you'll use only a monologue. However, a skilled celebrant will deliver it in such a way that you can imagine it as part of a dialogue. There'll be times throughout this book where the word dialogue is used for convenience (even though we're only hearing the words of one person).

The following extracts feature various literary elements. See if you can identify them.

> *If you were ever to reach into Lucy's pockets, you'd find they, like her, were full of sweetness. Secret stashes of sugar cubes nestled against her body. Those trademark pear-shaped thighs, so reminiscent of Rubenesque artwork, earned her the playful nickname of Wedge.*
>
> *This habit of carrying ample pocketfuls of sugar was for shared adventures with her granddaughter, Trina, so they could stop by paddocks and let horses nibble them from their hands. Although she was the ever-doting grandmother, truth was that Lucy's love of*

animals was so great that she'd have fed the horses anyway whether Trina was with her or not.

We have <u>scene setting</u>: we can imagine Lucy and Trina at the paddock and the horses nibbling from their hands.

There's <u>character</u>: Lucy is sweet, like the sugar. She's kind; and an animal lover.

We have <u>imagery</u>: if we've never met Lucy we know that she has large thighs. Her nickname shows that she was comfortable being identified in that way.

I could have just written: *Lucy and her granddaughter loved to feed the horses sugar cubes.* Can you see how different this makes the eulogy when you move from telling a few facts to creating a story?

> *Lucy began employment as a typist in Carlisle. Rarely did she talk about the job, but more the story of how she was always late catching the train from Lazonby to Carlisle, and how everyone in the office would watch her running in late, gasping for air and apologising. Despite this, Lucy secured the job until she began married life.*

We learn about her employment, and more about her character. Perhaps timekeeping wasn't a great skill? She certainly made an impression in the office by rushing in. Maybe she wasn't overly reliable about starting on time. And yet, she maintained her job. We also learn a bit about the history of the time: Women only worked until marriage.

> *Heading straight to the coin-operated Kiddie Ride at the supermarket was yet another opportunity for Lucy to bestow nurturing on her young granddaughter. It was with joy that she'd obligingly pop in a silver 20p coin for Trina to ride the mechanical horse. A simple coin. Yet so much fun! When the ride inevitably came to an end, Lucy would say "Oh go on, Trina, have another go!" And in would go another coin. This love of play was all very well, but there are only so many times a child can gallop on one of those things without getting dizzy!*
>
> *Life doesn't wait for anyone. Days turn to years. Little girls soon grow up and become women. Lucy kept up the tradition of saving 20p coins for Trina right up into adulthood, not for the Kiddie Rides but so that Trina could use them at university in the campus clothes dryers.*

In the above paragraphs we see Lucy as a doting grandmother. There's <u>scene setting</u>, <u>dialogue</u>, <u>character</u>. We also see the <u>passage of time</u>: witnessing her granddaughter as a young child and becoming an adult.

Dee

If you wanted to see Dee at her happiest, you only had to take a peep at her on the dance floor as she jived. The dance style suited her personality perfectly for it is uninhibited, happy, boppy and energetic, with all that bending, rocking of the hips and knee lifting. By far the fastest of the Latin dances, there are plenty of kicks and flicks and at speeds between 128 and 176 beats a minute. And that was Dee: a woman who simply couldn't sit still.

Again, I could have written that "Dee loved to dance" and left it at that. Instead, I compared the ridiculously fast beats of the jive to her personality. We learn about her physically *and* emotionally: she was happiest on the dance floor.

Vikki

When I met Vikki's daughters, they were clear about one thing: they did NOT like their mother. My heart sank. How was I going to write a eulogy for a woman about whom they had nothing nice to say? Reading between the lines, I felt it was more about them feeling unloved.

On the other hand, Vikki's friends adored her. I've had this particular scenario many times in my funeral-celebrant career: disliked by family, loved by friends and community. What I do is honour the perspective of the chief mourner/s without putting the deceased's memory down.

So, here's how I opened Vikki's eulogy:

> *Vikki said that "The best thing about getting older is that you can say what you want!" Like any human, Vikki was multifaceted. On one hand she shied away from attention and never liked to make a fuss and yet, on the other, she could be spirited and direct in her speech.*

I honoured the dual nature of her personality: she never liked to be in the spotlight but she also said what was on her mind. I've used dialogue to bring Vikki straight into the story. After all, she was direct in her speech so it was right that she opened the eulogy with her own words. I've also honoured the daughters by acknowledging that their mother's speech could be injurious to feelings, however, only they would hear that in those words. Anyone else in the audience would hear "direct in her speech".

Honesty is important. After all, we're here to remember who a person was in their lifetime. We all have our own perspective of the humans we come across (rightly or wrongly).

Adam
While Cherry was making me a cup of tea, I commented on a beautiful piece of art in the living room. It was of a kingfisher. Had I not commented and had the ensuing conversation, the following opening to (her husband) Adam's eulogy may never have come about. I could have just written: "Adam loved fishing".

> *If you ever, perchance, came across a solitary man beneath a starry night sky, standing knee-deep in the ice-cold waters of an English river, fishing rod in hand, it could well have been Adam Collins.*
>
> *This fondness for solitude and the natural world accompanied him his whole life. It was here, deep in the bosom of Nature, with the towering trees as guardians, the soothing waters slipping by and capturing his secret soulful thoughts, the shrill whistle of the kingfisher, and sanctity of pure air filling his lungs, that he found a comfort which was often denied him during his formative years.*

These paragraphs formed the foundation of his story: a childhood where he was denied the maternal influence of his birth mother, and again experienced maternal rejection from his stepmother. Fishing was more than a sport or hobby. It gave him: Nature. Comfort. Solace. It was only fitting, that after death, he had an eco-burial in an ancient woodland where he was able to rest in the safe arms of Mother Nature.

In two paragraphs we have <u>scene setting</u>, <u>character</u>, <u>imagery</u>.

Daphne

> *To see Daphne at her most creative, you only needed to step into her kitchen. Here you'd find her baking any sort of pie, tart or cake which would make the most of the fruits she'd grown,*

or eggs from her chickens. Blackcurrant cake, gooseberry or raspberry pie; lemon meringue or egg custard and plum cake.

With her close-knit family, Daphne enjoyed brambling down Warwick-on-Eden along tracks by farmers' fields. The kids would be able to go lower and deeper into the brambles to find their luscious plump fruits. Daphne would reward the family with her divine bramble cake. Without fail, her old pantry always had tins bursting with home-made cakes.

This ability to create abundance was forged from years of hardship and frugal living in which she mastered the art of taking minimal resources and crafting something delightful, decadent and delicious.

Pressed Flowers

Often in my funeral celebrant work, there is synchronicity at play. On the day I went to the hospice to meet Marsden's family, I'd been scrambling around my cottage trying to find a spare notebook. I have loads of notebooks but it's always a matter of finding one which still has plenty of blank pages left in it. I picked one up, and no sooner had I opened it, did a whole bunch of pressed flowers fall out. *Oh no*, I thought. *That's no good. I can't have pressed flowers falling over the hospice floor.* Turns out it was a sign!

Marsden

> *Pressing flowers was a quintessential pastime in the Victorian era that can be traced back to ancient Egypt. Marsden enjoyed the beauty and pleasure of this simple hobby, and appreciated the important part it played in botanical history when plants were collected and preserved by travellers and botanists. Pressed flowers adorned his home.*

We learn both that it is a pastime which goes back a long time, and that Marsden enjoyed this hobby.

> *A man of wanderlust, possessed of a truly free spirit, Marsden strolled through this world wearing his own shoes, and ambling along to the beat of his own drum. And those hiking boots were ones he was incredibly comfortable in. Right size, right look and right make.*
>
> *A handcrafted, colourful and vibrant life, steeped in passionate pursuits, Marsden passed from this world with no regrets.*

These were the two opening paragraphs of Marsden's eulogy. We immediately get the sense that he was different to other people.

> *The richness of his days can't possibly be measured by the standards of the common man. Each day he experienced sheer joy by honouring the sacred details of those things he found beautiful. Not for him was the world*

> *of material gain and ambitions. Rather, he invested his heart and soul into embroidering each day with the magic and mysteries of the natural world.*

Again, how different was Marsden's life from the average person working nine to five? A mourner should never be in any doubt about whose funeral they're at. Marsden's character shines through here.

> *A sociable introvert, Marsden would always greet you with "Hello darling" or "Hello sweetheart". That natural tendency to be so kind, warm and friendly was no doubt due to his innate awareness of when it was time to go Walkabout.*

In the above paragraph, he is 'brought to life' by introducing some dialogue which highlights his friendly character.

> *Solitude was his touchstone, and here he'd find the soul nourishment that enabled him to then give more fully to his friends and family upon his return. Marsden enjoyed fantastic friendships, and they were important to him throughout life. This uncanny ability to pick up any relationship from just where he'd left off before disappearing remained with him throughout life.*

What do you learn about Marsden from the above paragraph?

> *The simple life always lured him towards the great outdoors, and the hills called to his soul in a way nothing else could. After gathering some essentials in his backpack, he'd jump on his bike, and vanish for days.*

Through his actions: jumping on his bike and heading to the hills, we learn more about who he was.

Let's see if we can physically identify Marsden.

> *Easily spotted in a crowd by his crown of long, luscious curly hair, Marsden would unselfconsciously amplify his presence by carefully etching on eyeliner, donning his flamboyant clothes, and strolling down the street with a cane in his hand.*

> *This adoration of beauty extended from the natural world to the clothes he wore, and his own body, one that was particularly tanned, toned and taut throughout adulthood.*

It's not necessary to include someone's physical appearance in a eulogy, but there are times when it also highlights their character in some way (as the above narrative shows). We've already learned that Marsden was an independent chap, and liked to do things his own way. Here's a glimpse into his freedom-loving self.

> *Just securely over the cusp of adulthood, it was at the age of twenty when Marsden stepped out the door to buy a pack of cigarettes. A year*

> *later, he came home. Somehow he'd ended up in India! Ever interested in the world around him, Marsden would always take the longest possible route when he travelled just so he could see more. Ever curious, he simply had to know what was around the corner, over the hill, and beyond the horizon.*

So, from the above paragraphs we learn Marsden was spontaneous. I could have just written "Marsden was a spontaneous man!" Would you, or any of the mourners in the audience that day, have remembered he was a spontaneous man if I'd said that? Maybe, but you're more likely to remember it by his wee diversion to India! I know, for me, I shall never forget that part of his life's story. We know he was a man of adventure but the following extracts show he was also a man of intellect, with deep values.

> *Diligently earning degrees in art and geology, these were simply to augment his deep fascination for beauty, excavation and solidity. Work was the last thing on his mind.*

> *Not at all career minded, instead he'd rather jump on his bike, carrying a one-man tent, and follow the road.*

We learn more about his character: determined, dedicated and disciplined (not one degree, but two); but also there's a glimpse of imagery by having him in action: jumping on a bike, and tent on his back.

Marsden was born to be free. With his head often in a book, his curiosity and intelligence led him to be a man who knew an awful lot. You sensed that his mind and heart were like a rich seam of precious metals embedded deep inside the earth. With his satchel hanging over his shoulder, it faithfully contained a book, a notepad, pen and pencils. Marsden was never without the little hammer he used for working with fossils; not to mention the magnifying glass that he kept to hand. This allowed him to study things in great detail.

Always one to sketch and write down thoughts in his diary, Marsden was also drawn to collecting quality notebooks.

In the above paragraphs we learn that even though he hasn't used his degrees in art and geology to earn an income, they were integral to how he lived his life: infused with a deep love of beauty, curiosity and exploration.

There was an inner contentment and curiosity to Marsden which was captured on the pages he sketched upon, and the canvases his paint brushes would imbue with colour. These skills crossed from fine art to abstract, but whatever path his art followed, he was clear about one thing: he refused to make money from his art, insisting it was a gift.

Home was a living testament to his great loves: art, beauty, rocks, stones, pressed flowers, colour and literature. No gaps on walls or shelves existed, such was his shrine to a life well lived. They feature sentimental items from all over the world. A man of exceptionally good taste, and a wonderful conversationalist, Marsden could talk to you long, long into the night, and you'd never grow tired. Marsden lived in Europe, hitchhiked across Syria, explored India, and hiked the Himalayas. The kind of person who seemed to know something about everything, every conversation would leave you richer. Marsden was kind, friendly and gave "a bloody good hug".

Tell Marsden's Story
Taking the raw facts from Marsden's life, write three paragraphs of a eulogy for him.

Themes and Cinematic Views

When I'm going through my notes after a funeral family visit, I look at the themes of the deceased's life. After I type up my notes (just as I've written them in my book), I then add bold headings for the themes of their life. I then cut and paste my material into the relevant sections. This alone can take an hour or two. It's not uncommon for mentions of a theme (e.g. cooking) to come up several times in a conversation. My chief mourner/s may mention an aspect of cooking five minutes into our conversation, then again at 10, 20, one hour in, and so on. I then bring all of these mentions into the same section.

So there's all this work (preparation) before I even start writing! What it does do is allow me to really think about who this person was, and what was important to them. Once I've decided my opening scene, I then have to find a way to 'link' the themes. For example, themes from my own life story would include:
.nature
.solitude
.classical music
.plant-based cooking
.gardening
.love of home
.childhood on a horse stud in rural Australia
.world travel
.deep love of family

.writing
.reading (magical realism, chick lit, romance novels, any vegan, vegetarian, gluten-free recipe books, gardening, mind/body/soul, writing, abundance, alternative health, celebrancy)
.psychological astrology

After I've written a eulogy, I remove the bold 'theme' headings. They're only in my script as guidance or scaffolding while I write the first draft.

Nancy
Food, in particular cooking, was a huge theme in Nancy's life story and came up many times in the family meeting, so it warranted several paragraphs.

> *If you stopped by Nancy's house for a cup o' tea, you'd step into her busy kitchen where every single surface groaned under the weight of all her baking. Now, it has to be said, she wasn't necessarily the best baker in town but she was almost certainly the most passionate.*

> *A dusting of flour upon her cheeks, oven mitt in hand, Nancy produced the most handsome batch of pasties. They'd rest upon the kitchen table, already laden with an entire bakery of cakes; and the benches simply had no room to spare.*

> *The memories of food made with love, nourish us just as much as what we ate at the time. Feeding you was Nancy's way of saying she*

cared. One of her neighbours once commented that he liked cakes. Since that day, Nancy never stopped baking for him!

If Nancy woke up at 2am, insomnia dragging her by the heels from under the bedcovers, she'd slip down to the kitchen and the baking day would begin in earnest.

Each cake she baked had a little story behind it, such as the apple-and-blackcurrant pie she'd serve up. Mysteriously, it had no apple. And the hangover cure sure to fix you: her infamous cheese-and-onion pasties. Delicious! Um, except for one small detail: there was no cheese! And what of the mouthwatering lemon cake which was actually an orange cake?

Incorporating cinematic views means being conscious of imagery to evoke feelings. Scene setting, however, isn't just about what we see; it's also what we *hear*, *touch*, *taste* and so on. There are other senses, too, such a thermio-ception (temperature). How can we weave these into our stories?

Angus
Such was his hearty appetite for life that Angus naturally wanted to share everything he'd learned, whether it was by showing an experiment in front of a classroom of eager young faces, sharing an adventure high up in the mountains, or the simple pleasure of growing a plot of potatoes. This generosity of

spirit stayed with him from childhood to the end of his days as a doting grandfather.

Can you see the faces of the kids in his classroom looking on enthusiastically? Can you imagine Angus picking tatties? We get a glimpse into his joy as a mountaineer, and there's also a time signature.

Ace

Ace marvelled at words. They were his way of exploring this world, of understanding new ideas, and sharing information with those around him. A jovial chatterbox, he had the ability to talk to anyone about anything. Whether it was a subscription to Navy Monthly or reading The Guardian while enjoying his boiled egg and cup of tea each morning, words gave him a passport.

Character Identification

Whether you're writing a novel or writing a eulogy or a love story for a wedding, character identification is key: it leads to intimacy in our storytelling.

Think about when you've read a novel, and regardless of whether it's the protagonist, antagonist or a random secondary character, the reason you connect with them is because you can identify with something about them. It can be the smallest of things: the smattering of freckles on their face, or the way they always pull the beetroot out of their burger, or how they donate their Christmas gifts to a charity or dance in the rain.

In our storytelling, we seek to find ways to help the reader/listener *connect*. Often, in my funeral work, I'll come across a life story for which I have no connection (e.g. they spent all their time at the pub, a bingo hall, or in a shooting range. Maybe they beat pheasants or set traps for rabbits.). My job (and yours, if you're writing their eulogy) is to inhabit that world; to feel their passion. To understand what drew them to it. You can probably imagine that, as a person who chose to become a vegetarian at the age of five, and worked as a media officer for an animal-welfare charity and an animal-rights charity, I have to work doubly hard on any story which involves animal deaths, torture or cruelty.

It's never enough to say "(name) did this" or "did that". We need to *show* them actively engaged in their pursuits and discover how others might relate to some aspect of the person. It might be that they connect to the person's 'thrill of the chase' or 'detective skills' or 'jubilation at winning' or 'circle of companions'. Can you see how this shifts things? We illustrate what was meaningful to them, and look at the 'why' of that particular interest.

*Character identification
leads to intimacy
in our storytelling.*

In the previous eulogy extract, you're at the breakfast table with Ace as he flicks through the newspaper. We don't have to share the same hobbies, interests, career or lifestyle as the deceased to be able to relate to them, but we can connect in other ways: boiled egg or cup of tea? Reading the newspaper? How about words as playthings? We rely on them to navigate this world. Character identification leads to intimacy in our storytelling.

Justin

Justin was a shining light in his community, infusing all those around him with warmth, enthusiasm and creativity. Always on the go, brimming with vitality, if there was a job to do or someone needed to be inspired, Justin was the one person you could definitely count on.

Driven to ensure his village of (name) was a vibrant and thriving place to live, it was inevitable that he ended up on various committees, for these are hubs of action and progress. If you ever had a question about a village matter, you'd be told "Ask Justin!" for he simply knew every last detail. An example of his dedication, commitment and investment in steering matters in the right direction could be found through his involvement in raising money for the new village hall. Alongside this, he enjoyed being a member of the local quiz league, helped with the parish church, and village conservation group.

Have you come away from that glimpse into Justin's world with a strong sense of what was important to him? *Community.*

Jake

If ever there was a man who believed in himself, it was Jake. And his life was a testament to his strong sense of identity, and his ability to confidently navigate the world whether it was in sales or sailing, wearing bike leathers or jodhpurs, or cantering along The Common. Through trial and error, but mostly forged from a love of adventure and risk taking, Jake created an amazing life for himself.

The most accurate word to describe him would be charismatic, but of course, like any human, Jake was a deeply composite character, and those who knew him intimately were well versed in his ability to be both chalk and cheese. A complete charmer, he derived huge pleasure as a storyteller, however his tendency to share stories at enormous length, not just once, but many, many times over, often had those closest to him begging "Can we have the short version please?"

When I arrived at Jake's home for the family visit, I was in for a real surprise. The family were quick to tell me that they didn't even want a funeral for him. One family member said, every minute or so throughout the entire meeting, "He was a real sh*t";

and less often, but still quite regularly, another family member said "He *really* was a sh*t!" After some time, I put my pen down and said (inwardly groaning with exasperation) "You know what? One thing I'm *really* good at is writing 'He was a sh*t!' You'll hear that, but nobody else will unless, of course, they also know this as their truth!" The energy in the room shifted, and I could tell they trusted me to do the job.

The funeral was heaving with people. The man had been well known and popular (just not so popular with his own family). After the ceremony, the mourners piled out, laughing, and said "You really summed him up accurately!"

Laurie

For Laurie's eulogy, his love of water and family needed to shine from the script.

> *Water, words, and the womb of family life, all describe the most meaningful things and experiences Laurie enjoyed. A man who thrived by being near water, whether it was a stroll in the glorious summer sunshine around Talkin Tarn near Brampton, or diving into the ice-cold waters of the North Sea in the middle of a freezing winter, he made sure never to be too far away from it. There was something about the freedom of being in and around water that he found exhilarating and emotionally nourishing, and throughout his life continued to draw sustenance from it.*

Walking along a sandy beach, the crash of the waves in his ear, and his beloved family by his side, was all Laurie really yearned for in life. An ideal holiday for him was on the south coast, particularly places like Dorset, exploring various villages and discovering new coastal paths, as well as ambling alongside canals where he could stop off for a pub lunch on the way.

*Our dead are never dead to us,
until we have forgotten them.*
~ George Eliot

Writing Tips

Time Signatures

Time signatures offer us a way to show time without necessarily using dates or the hands of the clock. Here are a few examples. The first was from Rex's ceremony. Rex was a real party animal, and the ultimate festival goer. We'd just come out of the pandemic and were slowly being released from restrictions. This is the opening paragraph:

> *This is the biggest party Rex has been to for the past two years! Imagine the pleasure he'd have had knowing that we're wearing vibrant colours and that the LED lights are glowing. Though, if he'd arranged it himself, this would be no less than a full-blown festival.*

There was no need to mention the pandemic or lockdowns. The fact I said it was the biggest party he'd been to for two years said everything that needed to be said. We all knew: we'd been locked away for far too long!

> *"I've had a bloody good life!" Annabel said. From start to end, she had a way of creating a life that was true to her talents and desires, and innately knew how to have fun. A woman who danced through every era, and loved rock*

> *'n' roll and jiving, she'd eventually teach her daughters the joy of spinning around the dance floor.*

What do we learn in the opening paragraph of Annabel's eulogy? She's not a young woman: she's danced through every era. She's a mum, and she taught her daughters to dance. We learn a lot about her through this time signature.

See what time signatures you can find in the following paragraphs about Isaac's life.

> *That Isaac even had a chance to live his amazing life is nothing short of a miracle. Due to his father's service in the jungles of Burma during the war, he'd been declared infertile. So, when Isaac's mother, a nursing assistant, discovered she was pregnant, not just with one child but with twins, it was a shock to everyone. Wartime was not an easy start to life. Imagine their mother trying to obtain a double pram with coupons?*
>
> *Life began in a one-bedroom cottage the family shared with their granny. They never met their grandfather, who'd been a cobbler, and had cobbled in the front room.*

When was the last time you heard of someone being a cobbler? Might that be a time signature as well as imagery? And how about the sense of time where a family lived in a one-room cottage?

> *Home was in Bisham. It was an idyllic childhood of stretched-out days, exploring hundreds of acres of the ancient woodland on a hillside rising from the floodplain of the River Thames. A whole gang of kids would disappear for the day, only returning home when their tummies growled. Alongside the hoot of the tawny owl, Isaac and the other kids climbed trees, constructed dens, and set up camp. At harvest time, their camps were made from hay bales.*

Do you remember the days when kids would just head outside all day long and not return home till it was time to eat? Perhaps this has two time signatures, then. 'Back in the days' when kids played outside and built things rather than being glued to a phone screen; and the day itself: dinner time.

Pronouns

As a celebrant, I'm acutely aware of the use of pronouns and ensuring that I'm using the preferred pronouns of the clients I work with, but I also have another view of pronouns, and that is in my storytelling. I use them sparingly when starting sentences. Why? Because when they're a crutch, it leads to lazy writing.

If you're a working celebrant, why not examine some of your scripts and see how you fare? Circle or highlight every sentence which starts with a pronoun. When a eulogy has a lot of them it sounds like a shopping list; aka boring.

To be clear, a pronoun is a substitute for a noun. It is a short word: he, her, him, his, I, me, us, we, you, who, themselves, each other.

> *Jack Smith was born in Manchester on the 4th July 1972. He lived with his mother, Jane, and five brothers. His home was on Elm Street, just over the road from the cricket club. He learned to play there.*

Surprisingly, many eulogies are written with this proliferation of pronoun-starting sentences. Not only does it lead to lazy writing, it also reduces the writer's ability to be creative. These sentences often lack rhythm or imagination, hence the feel of a shopping list. When spoken, they're boring and it's a quick way to send an audience to sleep.

Relative Pronouns
Who refers to people.
Which and *that* refer to things and animals.

Who is the subject of the sentence.
Whom refers to the object of a verb.

Very

'Very' is another word I work to eradicate from the scripts of my celebrants-in-training. Why? This word is rarely needed. It is almost always used for emphasis because the writer doesn't feel that the word which follows it is strong enough. I would encourage you to question each word you use. Can you find a stronger word?

Here are some examples:
You could say "very angry", or how about: seething, incensed, furious, outraged, enraged or livid?
Very boring: dull, tiresome, pedantic, tedious?
Very bad: terrible, awful, horrible?
Very bright: dazzling, brilliant, radiant, luminous?
Very beautiful: gorgeous, exquisite, ravishing, lovely, stunning?
Very large: enormous, huge, colossal, massive, gigantic?
Very clean: spotless, immaculate, gleaming, pristine?
Very cold: freezing, frosty, arctic, frigid?

To be clear, it's not that the words angry, boring, bad, and so on, are wrong; it's the questionable use of the word 'very'. To feel the need to use it means that the word following it isn't strong enough for you. Once you become aware of things like this, you'll learn to self-edit with ease and confidence. It will make all the difference to your eulogy writing.

Develop Your Skills

In the list below, there's an example of a word that could be used. Write two of your own.

1. Very competitive. *Cutthroat*
2. Very deep. *Profound*
3. Very crowded. *Bustling*
4. Very dirty. *Filthy*
5. Very different. *Disparate*
6. Very easy. *Effortless*
7. Very empty. *Desolate*
8. Very colourful. *Vibrant*

Sadly

Another word I'm challenged by in storytelling (especially in celebrancy) is the use of the word 'sadly'. It's often used to short-circuit a difficult story. It's like we're saying, "Yep, that was sad, let's skip over it!" The word 'sadly' is often, at best, ambiguous.

Sadly, Brian's wife died of cancer.
Sadly they divorced.
Sadly, their only child died.
Sadly, he lost his job.
Sadly, the house was burnt down.

As a creative writer, offering an emotional lens, don't tell the audience something was sad. *Show* them. In doing so, you'll allow the person listening to 'complete the circuit' without telling them how to feel. Here are some examples:

> *Baby brother Jamie was lovingly welcomed into their home, his gurgles and giggles lighting up their days. Dave's first experience of grief came to him early in life when Jamie passed away at just six months of age.*

I haven't shied away from the fact that his adorable baby brother died. It also shows that grief came to Dave's life early on. There'd be three major grief stories in his life: his baby brother, his own child, and that of his wife.

> *Life brought unimaginable tragedy, and they were forced to grieve the stillborn death of*

> *their only child. As is often the case, theirs was a silent grief they endured primarily on their own, shared only with close family. Their loving and devoted relationship to each other gave them the comfort and solace to survive and forge a future together; one which was completely different to the life they'd imagined.*

How different does this sound to 'sadly their only child died'? We learn that they were forced to grieve. And we learn, as is often the case with miscarriages and stillbirths, their mourning was done away from others. By not limiting myself to 'sadly', I have the opportunity to show that this couple's bond was strong, and though their lives were completely different than the one they'd hoped for, they survived. It's a story of triumph over tragedy. We do a disservice to the person whose story we're telling when we skate over difficult topics with the word 'sadly'.

When a well-known and popular man in my community died, it would have been easy to focus the majority of his eulogy on his career (after all, that's how most people knew him). What I learned was that their only child had been killed, and his death led to other changes in their life. Perhaps you can now see that "Sadly Aidan died at the age of fourteen" just doesn't cut it.

> *Sometimes life brings events or situations which come from left field and throw us off course. For this closely embroidered family,*

an emotional earthquake forever changed the landscape when young Aidan's life ended abruptly while climbing in the Lake District. Aidan was just fourteen years old.

Utterly heartbroken, knowing life would never - could never - be the same again, Kevin and Amy took up a friend's suggestion to move to a little village, just a few miles out of the city. With heavy hearts, they packed up their family home, and that same year moved to Bramble Cottage, by the River Eden.

Alongside the perpetual silent scream which now penetrated their days and nights, their new home brought a wealth of life-enriching experiences. Living beside the rattling sound of the railway tracks meant waving at the passing steam trains, meeting new people in the village and forging friendships, and breathing in the fresh morning air that rural living offers.

A few years after their move, another event would prove to change their lives. Kevin and Amy were able to buy a field behind their home. And here, on these twelve acres, they began planting a woodland in Aidan's memory.

The eulogy then continued with a descriptive walk of the woodland they planted; and the incredible legacy they've created in their son's memory

> **What Does 'Sad' Look, Sound & Feel Like?**
> If you find yourself writing 'sadly' in a eulogy, ask yourself why.
>
> If you're a celebrant, why not explore some scripts where you've written 'sadly', and rewrite those sections by showing the situation and emotional tone?

Show Don't Tell
Although it would take exceptional skill to 'show' rather than 'tell' all the way through a eulogy, if we can bring more consciousness to our writing it will transform the body of work we produce. The concept of 'show don't tell', while a simple one, takes practice and more practice. Here are some examples:

Tell: Josh was a tall man.
Show: Josh always had to duck when he went through a doorway.

Tell: Frank was an accountant.
Show: Frank forbade his secretary from disturbing him throughout the last week of January. The door remained locked as he filed the tax returns of his notoriously late clients. By the first of February, he was at Heathrow heading off to the Bahamas.

What's more powerful?
1. There was a dog in the garden.
2. A blood-covered Scottish Terrier dug up Grandma's rose garden.

Showing is about imagery (visual, auditory, and so on) and *action*. It's also about detail.

When I asked Oscar's wife, Delilah, what she'd remember most about him, her answer surprised me. Her husband had been well known, due to his career, by so many people. I expected her to say something in relation to that. Instead, she replied "his pipe".

> *Those who knew Oscar well, considered him to be a deeply patient man. Perhaps the secret can be found in his morning ritual. Upon waking, Oscar stepped outside in his dressing gown, with a mug of steaming tea, a bowl of warming porridge, and his trusty pipe.*
>
> *Smoking a pipe is an ancient, leisurely and manly art. You need a good twenty minutes or so. It's a ritual as much as a form of relaxation. Oscar would pack his pipe with monochromatic walnut flakes, and delighted in its slow-burning properties, and full-bodied rich and distinctive scent. First, there was the familiar whoosh sound of the match lighting it, followed by the sweet earthiness mixed with a woody molasses aroma.*
>
> *With Homer, the chocolate Labrador, nearby wagging his tail, Oscar created a calm day ahead with this daily time for reflection.*

> **Scratch That Itch!**
> The following examples *tell* you something.
> Rewrite them so they *show* that:
>
> Pam had eczema.
> Granny was a cook.
> Jeff's wife died.
> They heard the train go by.
> There were clouds overhead.

A Sensual Life
Our ability to show more in our writing is enhanced by developing our skills regarding the sensuality of being human.

We're all familiar with the five senses:
.sight or *vision*
.hearing or *audition*
.smell or *olfaction*
.taste or *gustation*
.touch or *tactition*

We quite possibly take our senses for granted, until they're taken away.

Following a bout of covid, Stacy could no longer smell or taste. As an avid cook, this was enormously frustrating. Without these senses, appetite disappears completely. Where's the pleasure in eating if you can't taste the flavour or breathe in the aroma? It was a long and slow process to 'retrain' her senses.

Each day she'd gather her essential-oils collection, and breathe them in. "This is lavender", she'd tell herself, even when she couldn't detect anything. There'd be jasmine, ginger, peppermint, and so on. Her world felt hugely lacking. As she breathed in the essential oil of lemongrass, she reminded herself of how, in childhood, her mother would gather fresh lemongrass leaves and steep them in a pot of tea.

When a young friend of mine was in primary school, she was in a stationer's shop one day when she noticed a girl trying to find something. The staff member was becoming irritated as they didn't understand the girl's request. She was deaf. My friend was moved by this. The next day she asked her school teacher if the class could learn sign language.

Is There Something Missing?
How often do we seek to understand another?

Do you or someone you know not have full use of a sense or senses? How has it changed how you/they experience life?

Write three paragraphs, eulogy style, exploring this.

Body Awareness

Proprioception is about body awareness. Close your eyes, and then touch your nose with the index finger of your right hand. How about your little finger of the left hand? *That's proprioception in action.*

The thymus gland is also known as our happiness gland. It can be found in the little dip between your clavicles. If you tap it for a minute or more, it changes the whole energy in your body. Try it! It's a great way of changing your mood or allowing yourself to be in a much better place for working with others. Why not let this become a regular habit? It's easy to do when you're waiting at a red light.

The Heart Smile is another good body-awareness exercise. Close your eyes, and imagine that your smile is happening across your chest. Let that smile grow and grow until it stretches out of your body, and is wider than your room, your home, your town, your country and so on. It changes your body chemistry when you engage in such an exercise.

Are there more than five senses?
Some neurologists believe we have nine senses.

What about our *sense of colour* or *sensitivity to air* or *wind pressure* or *our sense of balance or motion*? Have you ever been car sick? I can not cope as a back seat passenger. And I would never have survived a seven-week trip by sea. How about you?

What about the chemical senses, such as hunger or pheromones? Have you been the victim of a man's gorgeous aftershave? There are some that make me go so weak at the knees and my response has nothing to do with the person wearing it. That clearly goes beyond the sense of smell.

How about the mental senses, such as those of self, psychic ability, and so on?

Extrasensory: I was once driving through Cornwall along a quiet country lane when suddenly I was overwhelmed by a feeling that someone had died. As I turned the corner, there was an ambulance and car-crash scene.

I almost always know when my favourite funeral director is going to call me with a funeral booking. How? The word funeral comes into my head. Now, this might not seem like an unusual thing, given my occupation, but I don't have it happen with other funeral directors. One time, I was typing a message on my phone to a friend when the words 'Tracy is going to phone you with a funeral' came into my head, and within seconds (seconds!) her name appeared on the screen alerting me to the incoming phone call.

Recently, I was driving to a funeral and I heard the words "watch out for the deer" when suddenly a deer bounded out of the bushes across the road in front. A few weeks later, when I was driving along one of the quiet rural roads where I live, I was reflecting on that incident, and a voice said "watch out for the dog". I slowed right down, and as I turned the corner…there were two dogs.

The clairgifts:
clairaudience (clear hearing)
clairvoyance (clear seeing)
clairsentience (clear feeling)
clairsalience (clear smell or taste)

The clairgifts are senses, and yet most people don't experience them.

Extrasensory Experiences

Have you ever had an *extra*sensory experience? How did you experience it? A voice? A sense? A vision? A taste or smell? A knowing?

Do you know someone who has a clairgift? Maybe you've been to a clairvoyant who could see into your future?

Could there be even more senses?
Michael J. Cohen is an eco-psychologist who has identified about 53 senses. That takes our sensual experience of life to a whole new level! All of these senses help us to survive and thrive. If you consider that in the modern world, for example in the USA, many people live 95% of their lives indoors. Think about that for a moment. Imagine, for example, that you don't regularly experience the wind against your face or rain on your skin. Perhaps you're in temperature-maintained environments most of the time. How does your body deal with freezing weather or a heatwave when outdoors?

Example: When I was a child, we had a post-and-rail fence around the orchard. It was about 1.5 metres high. I loved walking along the top rail. Did you know that many of today's Western children can't even balance on a log that's on the ground? Balance is a sense. In old age, it is recommended that you regularly stand on one leg (and with your eyes closed, if you can manage it) to maintain the sense of balance.

Synaesthesia
Have you heard of synaesthesia? It is the *merging* of the senses such as when the brain doesn't separate them between our taste and sight. Another way of looking at it is *consciousness*. Some people *see* sound. Or can *taste* the green in an olive or see the letter h in green. My daughter, a musician and composer, has synaesthesia. It's impossible for her to see a musical note without seeing a colour.

> **Beyond the Veil**
> As a eulogy writer, consider how your writing might change if you're able to describe a person's life beyond their five senses?
>
> Once you become aware of just how many senses we have, you'll be discovering them everywhere you go, all day long, and your writing will open up in ways you could never have imagined.

Enhancing our creativity

Our creative spirit is nourished when we put feeling into our observations. When we slow down, when we observe, we live life at a walker's pace. And we learn by experiencing. We become not only energy curious but energy aware. *Our life changes.*

We learn to experience the world in a radically new way. We create by looking at connections, and this stimulates imagination. A lot of people in modern culture spend upwards of ten hours a day looking at a screen. We become consumers of information rather than creators. There's little room for daydreaming, and yet the daydream state is essential for our imagination.

> ## Living More Deeply
> For one week, keep a sensuality journal. For now, you can focus on the familiar five senses.
>
> This will make you aware of the world around you, and your place in it. If you can do this for yourself, imagine how it will enhance the way you write about other people's experience of life?

Extract from my Sensuality Journal

Sight
Rain, garden, body, face, granddaughter and daughter's faces; bumblebee washing itself; photos of a friend's garden. Opening letters in the mail and recognising handwriting.

Sound
Woodpecker. Blackbird singing. Cry of a seagull. Sparrows squabbling. Computer hum. Central-heating gurgle as it starts up. Voice messages. Voice on Zoom. Owl hooting. Mozart on record player. Bumblebee buzz.

Touch
Swimming in warm water. Heat of the jacuzzi. Grass under my feet. Carpet under feet. Velvet sofa. Wooden table. Flower petals. Hug. Shower.

Taste
Royal Gala apple, crunchy peanut butter. Sweet potato and bean soup. Chicory cappuccino. Water. Pear. Kiwi fruit.

Smell
Nag Champa incense. Petrichor. Wild-rose deodorant.

Other senses
Energised. Happy. Satiated. Endorphins.

Friday
Hug with my daughter after 14 months apart (pandemic). Bear hug with her new boyfriend. Lunch in vegan café. Sound of people's laughter. Glaswegian rain. Flowers. Lavender latte. Listening to Taylor Swift for the whole two hours of driving.

A New Perspective
Thinking about your day so far, write down five things you experienced through your senses.

Now, choose one of them and write two paragraphs about it as if it were in a eulogy.

Time Travel
Smell allows us to travel in time, whether it's a scent, aroma, fragrance, pong or stench. The following smells immediately take me back in time:
Grass just cut; I'm five years old in sub-tropical Queensland. Eucalyptus, and I'm in my homeland walking through a forest in Tasmania with my mum after a storm.
Freesias: my mum grew them in our courtyard.
Cinnamon.
Maya Spanish soap that my mum used. My dad gave it to my mum when he'd come back from overseas.

Our *sense* of smell determines if something is a scent, fragrance, aroma, or a pong, etc.

The Incubator
Your body is an incubator for creativity. This is where your intuition comes from. So the more you *experience* and *observe* your senses, whether that's the basic five or dozens of them, the more you have to draw on, not only for writing ceremonies and creating rituals, but also for the unspoken sense of feeling what your client needs. You become highly attuned not just to your own energy but other people's.

Landscapes
We have landscapes in our mind. For example, I grew up in rural Australia, and spent many nights sleeping outside on the trampoline with my mum. There were mountains with eucalyptus trees and yellow-blossomed wattle trees. We had a spring-fed creek, and dams. I'll never forget the seven-year drought

> **Memory Lane**
> Write a list of five natural smells that take you back to childhood, and why.
>
> Ask a friend or family member about smells, scents, fragrances, aromas or stenches and pongs which transport them to childhood, then write a few paragraphs of biographical storytelling.

and how a simple crack in the parched soil, over time, became a gully.

Someone recently asked me what my perfect day was like. After a few moments, I said I live my perfect day most days. By consciously engaging with my senses, the ordinary day becomes utterly extraordinary. For example, as I type this paragraph Mozart is playing on the stereo, rain is splattering against the windows, the cats are curled up beside me on the sofa, incense wafts through the room. A mug of hot water with lemon and honey is within easy reach. I'm fully engaged with my experience. Isn't that what life is about? This is certainly what I look for when 'researching' a person's life.

> **A Dandelion in the Sidewalk**
> Write a page or two about a landscape (seascape, skyscape, cityscape) you know intimately, either from childhood or another time in your life. How does or did it impact you? Now write two paragraphs about this in the third person.

> **Perfect Day**
>
> Describe your perfect day, then write a few paragraphs in the third person.
>
> Ask someone you don't know well, such as a neighbour or random stranger at the bus stop (after some other conversation) about what they consider to be their perfect day. How might you write about that?

Windows

If you're ever stuck with a story, particularly the opening, what you need is a window. A window is like being able to step into a situation. Two ways that offer a window are to start with the word 'If' or 'Even though'. They act as a sort of leverage. Here are some examples:

> *If Jackson were in charge of his eulogy, it would start like this: Jackson Mason; The Man, the Myth, The Legend! But was this because he was always in high-vis clothing, big boots, had even bigger muscles, or because of his passion for wildlife?*

Here's another example:
> *Even though Stephanie was a ballerina, she longed to be a jockey.*

Can you see the see-saw effect that just happened?

If Jessica hadn't gone to Venice, she'd never have known the joy of falling in love.

What happened in Venice? That's what we want to know.

If it wasn't for that twinkle in his eye, and sense of humour, Cornelius may have had a completely different life story. Instead, his open-hearted way, warmth and friendliness, fashioned his days with companionship, pleasure and appreciation for the finer things in this world.

If Cornelius had been a grumpy sod, spewing acerbic words and scowling his way through life, he certainly wouldn't have been the well-loved and respected man he was known as. I've taken both a physical description (imagery) and character (sense of humour) to lead us through the window. Once inside, we learn that his warm personality was the foundation for a life surrounded by people, pleasure and beauty.

If Finn were here, he'd offer you a glass of John Smith's Original so you could enjoy that malty, bittersweet ale that he so loved. And while you savoured the slight fruitiness of the brew and its bitter aftertaste, he'd regale you with a story. Instead, today we're sharing stories about him.

> *A man with an expansive, warm and celebratory approach to life, Finn was happiest down at the pub, The Plough Inn, where he could share the craic with mates. A traditional pub, on Friars Road, it was here that Finn made himself right at home — even having his own glass and his own chair. Not many people can claim that feat at their local!*

Finn's eulogy was initially challenging for me to write. His whole existence was based at the pub. From the moment it opened each morning, to last drinks, he was there. My approach changed when I fully immersed myself in his world.

Charlotte

> *Even though poor health would dominate much of her adult life, Charlotte never ceased to generously share her charitable spirit. Unless we've lived our lives in constant pain or sickness, it can be hard to understand just how debilitating and life altering such a hardship can be. It's as if you don't even have ownership over your own body, and one thing is clear: there's no escaping it. Despite this, Charlotte's benevolent attitude to people and pets provided an anchor which enriched her days and nights. It amplified her natural tendency to sympathise with the plight of others, and her beautiful smile was always at the ready to make your day a brighter one.*

Immediately we're in Charlotte's world: pain, illness, and relentless discomfort; and yet look at what she gave to others. Kindness, sympathy, a beautiful smile, nurturing. Can you see the see-saw at play here? On one side, a woman with long-term sickness and on the other a woman who was kind.

I'm not suggesting always starting a paragraph or eulogy with 'if' or 'even though'. They can be useful windows, though. Here's another type of window.

Windows Into Working Life

The Dressmaker
Eloise couldn't feel the ends of her fingers anymore. The numbness was a constant and frustrating irony: fingers which once afforded her a living, and a damn-fine reputation, eventually let her down. How was it possible that her currency: bringing beauty into the world, was no longer commercial tender?

Who here had their wedding gown sewn by Eloise? If so, raise your hand.

From the day she left school, Eloise was immersed in the magical world of lace, taffeta, silk and sequins. Within a year or so, she'd already garnered a reputation as a fine dressmaker.

Ever since she was five years old, she knew that this was her dream: and each day, she'd study her mother at the sewing machine as she mended clothes for people in the village, and sewed dresses for all the girls who attended the chapel. Yes, Eloise knew what her life would look like.

Some gowns required thousands of beads, all sewn by hand. No room for error, and repetitive. Much of her work was produced in her upstairs sewing room, with views over the fellside, but some evenings she'd join her husband in the living room and stitch to the sound of the crackling fire.

The Window Cleaner
The slosh of water in buckets, a bundle of scrims to dry the edges, squeegees and mops, and, of course, the ladders. These were the tools of the trade. Every morning had the same rhythm, rain, hail or shine, as he packed his car with supplies.

Johannesburg didn't grow up expecting to be a window cleaner: he dreamed of going to university, and studying veterinary medicine. But life has a funny way of working out.

It had brought him love, more than once, and life had also taken it away. Johannesburg once said that the longest relationship of his life had been with a ladder: 30 years. That is, until that icy Winter's day when he fell off, landing on sandstone, hitting his head, and breaking several bones. His loved ones were clear about one thing: he was never allowed up a ladder again. After several weeks of recovery, he returned to window cleaning: ground floor only!

Contrary to what you might think, he never did look through the windows into people's homes, but kept focused on the window itself: enjoying the meditative state of emptying his mind. And if a homeowner happened to be around, and offered him a cuppa and biscuit, he'd delight in the chat, and regale them with his stories. Such a solitary job for a man with a sociable heart.

Loved
Love is beautiful, and denotes pleasure, passion, affection, connection and care. And yet it is such an over-used word, and a poorly used word in celebrant storytelling. Again, like the word 'very' or repetitively starting sentences with pronouns, to rattle off a list of passions or values under the banner of 'love' can lose the power of good storytelling.

For example:
Felicity loved tennis, loved reading and she loved fashion too. Felicity loved cats.

How about:
With her head buried in a Catherine Cookson novel, and her cat, Italics, snuggled on her lap,

Felicity turned down invitations to the pub until she reached the last page. It was the same every Friday evening. One more page, one more chapter. "I'll be there soon," she'd text her friends. And then, finally, with a sigh of satisfaction, she'd place the book to one side; then scour her wardrobe until she found just the right outfit. The little red number she found in a charity shop, or jeans and t-shirt? Most likely it would be the lime-green linen dress her late mother brought back from Italy.

At dawn, every Saturday morning, Felicity was the first one on the tennis court. Following her warm-up exercises, she'd flick the strings on her racquet and wait impatiently for Jess, her doubles partner, to turn up.

"She was kind"

It's not unusual in my funeral meetings to hear words such as 'she was kind' or 'he was lovely'. I always dig deeper. "In what ways was she kind?" I ask. I seek to find examples so I can illustrate this kindness rather than say the word kind. "How was she lovely?" How can I bring this person 'back to life' for the ceremony? I then learn: Cassie volunteered at the Soup Kitchen on Friday evenings, and donated blood every four months. Whenever someone in the community died, it was Cassie who'd start the phone tree and ensure casseroles were left at the newly bereaved's home each evening, just before dinner time.

What gives you a better sense of Cassie? She was kind? Or the examples of how she was kind?

Molly

Here's an example of a woman who was extremely sensitive to life, empathic and compassionate. Rather than say she was empathic, we see it through her actions and experiences of the world.

> *Love permeated every aspect of Molly's life. A natural propagator of flowers and trees, she tuned into Nature's abundance; and, in her own words: "just helped things along". It was in stillness, and tilting into the quiet of life, that Molly felt most at home. A gentle soul, who walked so lightly upon this Earth, she was happiest lying in the grass or listening to drops of rain against the leaves of trees. It was as if she recognised that both she and the natural world were one.*
>
> *So attuned was she to nature, that as a child Molly would sit on the beach and feel all the power and energy of the ocean coming towards her, cleansing and healing her whole being. Sand nestled between her toes, the plaintive cries of gulls on the sea breeze tugged at her heart, and in her hair clung the scent of the salt air. It was here, at the threshold between high tide and low tide, that she'd return to often in the last months of her life.*

Molly's depth of compassion was rare amongst humans. Protective towards any creature, she exuded a reverence for every living being, demonstrating that compassion is the highest form of spirituality.

Author Bob Thurman said "Until you have real compassion, you can not recognise love."

Imagine Molly, as a young girl, heading off to school far earlier than she needed to, with one sole mission: To gather all the worms off the tarmac so they wouldn't get killed by passing cars. Love is a verb: her caring actions defined Molly's essence, and the path which lay ahead of her: a lifetime of lifting others up.

In childhood, her home was right near to old bombsites that hadn't been built on. The cityscape of screeching sirens, the stench of vehicle fumes, and unforgiving concrete all around was a harsh environment for such a sensitive young girl who yearned to meet herself through the beauty of nature. Undeterred, she followed the inner call and actively sought out life wherever she could: the grass in a park, trees in a cemetery, a dandelion growing in the sidewalk, or a discarded autumn leaf on the pavement.

Upon finding a blackbird nest one day, she made it her job to bring them a tub of cornflakes every morning.

When a moth, which had been living in her bedroom, died, Molly sobbed. For this lonely little girl, the moth had been her friend.

Verb is King

Although when we're writing a eulogy we're telling someone's life story both through what they've experienced and their essential personality traits, we have to 'move' the story along. Adjectives may give colour with description, but action words are King! They give our stories feet to walk, skip, hop, jump, run or even to stand still as we look around.

Once we've written our draft, we then go back over looking for words which could do with sharpening, changing, flipping or enhancing in some way. For example, make a cake or *bake* a cake? Walk or stroll?

In the following extract, I've underlined action words which help move the script.

Not surprisingly, as someone who was so carefree, he delighted in <u>flying</u> kites, perhaps <u>wishing</u> for the same ability to <u>lift</u> up into the sky, to be <u>carried</u> on a breeze, rebelling against the <u>tether</u> and <u>pull</u> of gravity, and <u>skirting</u> the world just that bit out of reach.

Life without television freed him up for all manner of interests. Always <u>tinkering</u> under the bonnet of a car, he'd end up having something or other in bits on the kitchen table. Fascinated by how things work, Zander would *pull everything apart. Exasperated at the ensemble of stuff on her kitchen table, his mum would say "But I need to cook!"*

Like some mad professor, he had a whole world in the shed that no one knew about. It was a massive workshop space, utterly chaotic, but he knew where every last tool was.

Bob

Fires were lit on the beach, the sounds of wildlife recorded, and the discovery of new wildflowers. So many beautiful memories were handcrafted from their treasured times. Bob, Nell and Chrissy studied the landscape intimately: the hills and glens, the wildlife, and the history.

They'd dance at Cèilidhs, the traditional Scottish gathering featuring dancing and the playing of Gaelic folk music. Though it has to be said, Bob wasn't a good dancer.

To the uninitiated, the life of a vet sounds glamorous or maybe even fun. All those puppies and kittens to play with! Apart from the need to have, at the least, a clinical interest in animals, the reality is: long days based on utilising the knowledge and experience of animal biology, nutrition, physiology and microbiology. The work day of a vet involves neutering, confrontations with scared and aggressive animals, administering vaccinations, x-rays, dental work, and, of course, the soul-wrenching *task of <u>euthanising</u> someone's much-loved pet. A strong work ethic and interpersonal skills are essential. Bob had these in abundance.*

Zoe

Whether you knew her as Hampsy or Zoe, more than anything she was known as the Queen of Time. With her days set to the reliable and steady tick of a clock, Zoe had an innate sense of rhythm and routine; and she tilted her life towards the ever-moving second hand, for she knew that if you didn't watch out, life would slip away from you. In her words, "When you're dead, you're dead!" And so, she made every day count.

It was a well-timed life, whether it was based on catching the bus, meeting a friend, knowing when the bin men would rattle down the street, taking an apple pie out of the oven, or a weekly phone call.

Moment by moment, her life was embedded in a sense of structure, and from this she felt grounded in reality. It brought security to an uncertain world.

Ruben

Ruben could see a piece of rough wood, and with both his engineer's eye and an innate creative flair, would fashion a beautiful piece of art. Woodturning became an all-consuming pastime, and for twenty four years he created everything from vases, bowls, to a clock, lamp base and table. There was always a world to discover beneath the bark of a branch. What marks were underneath? What could he craft? At the back of the garden, in Mister's Shed, it was just Ruben, his lathe, hand-held tools and wood. This enjoyable hobby was perfect for Ruben: it appealed to his pleasure in problem solving. And then there was the tactile nature of wood, as well as working with his hands, and the beauty this craftsmanship brought to the eye.

Solitude in the shed eased him. It was a place of calm and creativity; his happy place where he could turn wood and experiment, too, by adding resin. If you were gifted one of his pieces, you have with you a real treasure.

Go through the above two examples, looking for action words. Think about the sentences if they didn't have those words.

This piece below, *Changing Places*, was written by my husband, Paul, about his father. Go through it and identify action words. The more you become familiar with identifying them, the more easily you'll start to include them in your own writing.

And so... 1953! It was memorable for two things: the coronation of Queen Elizabeth, and the relocation of the other Elizabeth (no longer Bessie), and her husband, from South Shields to Heckmondwike as Cemetery and Parks Superintendent. One small step for Harold, a giant leap for Harry.

Not everything was coming up roses. At that time, South Shields was (and is) an industrial town, but in a vastly different way to the heavy-woollen district of the West Riding of Yorkshire.

The family left behind beautiful beaches, the openness of the sea, and the romantic nature of big ships ploughing through the waters as they moved in and out of the Tyne where it becomes the North Sea... girded by the two long piers of South Shields and Tynemouth, each with a lighthouse at its end, keeping a watchful eye over the huge Norwegian ferries, cargo ships, and the trawlers which worked out of North Shields.

Contrast that with their new location right in the middle of the heavy-woollen industrial area, which was peppered with enormous mill chimneys belching out smoke which blackened the naturally cream-coloured sandstone buildings.

And their new home, while no longer a prefab, was a largish, cold, blackened-sandstone building at the bottom end of Heckmondwike cemetery.

> *And there was a huge difference between the local accent and the Tyneside one. For quite some time Elizabeth had difficulty understanding what was being said to her. Weerstabarn didn't mean "Where are you going" in South Shields; and an oil was not a hole.*

Making Your Words Work
The key to improving your writing is to be conscious of the words you place on the page rather than just trying to reach a word count. So you've done your fact gathering, and you've written your first draft using plenty of imagery to breathe life into your eulogy. What else can you do?

Have you ever seen a child with a stick? More often the stick is something else: a sword, a guitar, a shovel, an axe, a microphone, a fishing rod or a wand. They see beyond the stick, and so too should we see beyond the word. The child has brought the stick to life.

How do we bring our words to life? Firstly by considering them as containers, and by using them to show a story. Can we make our words dance on the page? Yes, I believe so. There are techniques, such as alliteration which can help you, too. The art of alliteration is when you have two or more words in a sentence which start with the same sound. It's a literary technique that works particularly well, as the listener or reader really takes notice of what you're saying. Remember the tongue twisters in school?; over-exaggerated forms of alliteration: *Peter Piper picked a peck of pickled peppers*. Why use alliteration?

Is it necessary? No, you don't have to use it. I choose to employ alliteration as it ensures that prose has a graceful and lyrical quality. Here are some examples:
Clearing the clouds
Winding its way westward
Susan's Saturday Singers
Rambling across the rocky ridge
Choked and chuntered in church
Coffee and conversation
Groaning in the graveyard

Develop Your Skills
Write alliterative sentences with the following words:
Tuesday
Symbol
Planet
Candle
Teatime
Blue
Doll
Flower
Sheep
Tricycle
Sunshine
Kitten
Weather
Rotten
Starlight
Warrior
Dynamite
Kingdom
Meadow

Content & Creative Writing

I remember a funeral director once preparing me for a 'chatty' client. During our phone conversation the FD said "You'll need at least half an hour for your visit!" I nearly choked on my cuppa. *Half an hour?* My average family visit is about two hours. Sometimes it's longer, but rarely is it as short as an hour. During this time, my job is to really get a sense of their loved one. Sometimes this is easy, and sometimes I bang my head in frustration. Although I've developed skills in writing a eulogy with little information, my preference is to have so much information that it takes superb editing skills to whittle it down.

When I leave the visit, and I'm driving home, I think about everything I've heard and allow the images to settle within me. What I'm looking for is the strongest image (memory) to come to the forefront. Sometimes I even start writing it in my head.
Who was this person?
What made their life meaningful?
What things, people or experiences brought them the most joy?
What challenges did they face? How did they overcome them?
What did they live for?

If I were to step into their life at some point, where would I have found them? Did they have regrets, and why?

These are the questions which guide me in how I'll open the eulogy. Essentially, what I aim to do is bring the mourners to a 'scene' which epitomises the deceased when they were alive. Sometimes this has proved challenging because my intuitive voice has been diametrically opposed to what my logical voice suggests. I always listen to my intuition even if a battle ensues! And each time I'm rewarded by a mourner who says it was 'spot on'.

Here are some extracts from eulogies I've written. Think about how different they'd have come across had I chosen to write in the traditional format of chronological order in a statement style.

Sally the Journalist
Sally was a collector of stories, a gatherer of information, looking for details, and then sharing that with others. Today, as we reflect on her life, it's our turn to tell her story.

Erica
Erica had an enviable life in so many ways. Why? Because she made every single day count and created a carefully tended life rich in meaningful pleasures, both solitary and in good company, such as her long daily walks up the River Caldew to Dalston, then taking the long walk home on the other side of the river. Erica continued this right into her eighties.

Renowned for her love of food, she took the basic sustenance needed by all humans, and turned it into a joyous and celebrated art form, whether that was baking gingerbread, coffee kisses, or preserving her famous bramble jelly. Erica was a keen brambler, and as her parting gift to you, you'll find a recipe on the back of the Order of Service.

Erica made the BEST scrambled eggs ever, though no one knows how or why. And she didn't leave her secret behind. With a great love of herbs, she was sure to always add chives from the garden to her scrambled eggs.

Sundays with Grandma were a regular and much-celebrated part of childhood for her grandchildren. Apart from baking, cooking and gardening, Erica could identify all types of birds. In fact, as an avid artist she'd often sketch birds.

Home was the meeting place for all of the family. Erica's life was enhanced by her dogs, Bruce and Jenny; knitting at 6pm each night while she watched the news; and the many activities she shared with grandchildren. One of those treasured memories was creating exquisitely scented perfumes from the herbs and flowers she grew, so that the grandchildren could dab them on their wrists.

Listening to your intuition

Suzie had held a historically significant role in the county, and so in my mind her ceremony would have to have a certain feel. However, after my meeting with her children, the overriding image I had of her was of a woman who drove way too fast. I simply couldn't get the image out of my head. It also epitomised her personality, and how she lived life: Fast! My logical brain said "No, you can't write that"; my intuitive side called back: "Watch me!" The family thought the eulogy summed her up perfectly.

Speedy Suzie!

To describe Suzie's 92 years upon this Earth in the space of a handful of minutes is an impossible task; for hers was a life bursting with vitality, passion, drive, adventure, and fuelled by the desire to make her community a better place.

You can tell a lot about a person by the way they drive a car. Suzie: heavy right foot, changing gears while going around corners. In a hurry to get somewhere. Living life to the full!

It was during her pregnancy with Eliza, way back in the early 1950s, that she learnt to drive and discovered the immense independence it afforded her.

Ten years ago, at the age of 82, she was caught speeding at Calley's Hill doing an outrageous 34mph! Suzie was ordered to do a speed-

awareness course. Some people mightn't admit to such a thing, but not Suzie! Oh how she loved every minute of it! Being such a sociable person, she found the interaction with fellow speedsters totally enlivening.

Independence was a defining theme in her life, and this was highlighted by the fact she was still driving at 91.

Patrice from the Perfumery
This opening was for a woman who was exceptionally kind, and also worked in a perfumery.

There are some people who, their whole life long, emit a beautiful fragrance. It's the scent of kindness. Patrice was one of those people. And like just the right perfume, she wasn't overbearing. Indeed, her floral undertones were a delicate blend of humour, generosity, and creative flair. If you care to close your eyes, you might just catch her scent lingering in the air.

The Beat of Hector's Drum
The cornerstone of Hector's life was rhythm. For more than fifty years, Hector sat behind a set of drums developing skills in dexterity, flexibility, speed and endurance.

With a deep respect for tempo and rhythm, the grip of sticks and stroke technique meant that each moment of music was complemented by his time changes and textures. Consistency and coordination were vital.

A Daisy A Day

If you wanted to see Daisy-Ann at her happiest, you need only have followed her into the garden. With dirt under her nails, sunshine warming her face, and pollen dusting her fingers, flowers enchanted her with their beauty, patterns and scents. Daisy-Ann had the gift of ensuring that the garden was always in bloom.

Throughout the seasons, her garden revealed the story of her pleasures: Daffodils in the springtime, the wallflowers, perennials with showy blossoms, herbaceous borders, and colourful flowers cascading from hanging baskets. Amongst her favourites were roses, fuchsias and geraniums.

If Daisy-Ann wasn't in the garden, she'd be curled up on the sofa enjoying a gardening magazine and dreaming about what she'd grow the following season. With her green fingers leading the way, her passion for gardening took Daisy-Ann to the Chelsea Flower Show, RHS flower shows, and botanical gardens.

Christophe the Climber

Christophe could have told you that when it comes to mountain climbing "the higher you go, the better the view"; and that walking teaches us to take life slowly. It is as simple as it is difficult: one foot in front of the other. If it hadn't been for his passionate pursuit of this pastime, he might never have known what it is to breathe in the scent of heather on the fellside, or hear the beck waters frolicking over stones and rocks.

Being so connected to the beauty of nature was both addictive and enlivening. Whether it was catching a glimpse of a fieldmouse scurrying beneath a bush, or seeing sunlight skim across a tarn, his hillside adventures satisfied his curiosity for experiencing life as fully as possible.

Saffia

Saffia knitted her way into our lives with such care and kindness, carefully tending every stitch as she administered the task of being the best friend and family member she could be. Saffia created a balance between investing in friends and family through quality time, and her determination to be independent. Through it all, she lived her best life.

Intensely creative, and with an acute attention to detail, she could knit a whole jumper in a single day. With a particular fondness for the Aran style, she'd gift these beautiful handmade chunky jumpers to friends and family no matter where they lived. With each stitch, she left a piece of herself in this world to be remembered.

When you wear one of her jumpers, it'll be like she's wrapped herself right around you. Saffia Starling, *her own label, was sewn inside each lovingly knitted item.*

What we have done for ourselves alone
dies with us;
what we have done for others and the world
remains and is immortal.

~ Albert Pike

Difficult Death Stories

Whether we come to write a eulogy as a celebrant, vicar or layperson, we must keep in mind that a person is more than their death story.

It's inevitable to be consumed by the emotional toll of death by suicide, murder, or an infant death. First and foremost, our job is to: *remember the life that was lived*, and to tell that story with care, passion and purpose.

There are times when we have to be mindful of our own bias and judgements; for example, if the deceased was a wife beater or paedophile, or was estranged from all friends and family.

Our job is not to judge, but to understand. We were all born someone's baby. No one ever knows what it is like to walk in someone else's shoes. We may imagine. We may empathise. But we'll never truly know.

Funerals for the 'Unclaimed'

Some of the most challenging eulogies to write are those with no family members or mourners; these are commonly called Pauper's Funerals. To be clear, it isn't necessarily that the person was a pauper. It's an unfortunate term commonly used to describe those funerals the state pays for. It has nothing to do with a person's finances but is to do with if anyone is taking responsbility for the funeral expenses.

From my perspective, whether there are 500 mourners at a funeral or only the funeral director in attendance, I give the ceremony 100% of myself. There are no shortcuts, and certainly no 'in and out' of the service in five minutes.

The following example required a lot of research and awareness of how this person's life unfolded. I had next-to-no information and no mourners or care-home staff members to talk to. I often have to rely on storytelling techniques to build a picture.

> *Born in Preston, this riverside city began as a village called Priest's Tun, which means priest's farm. It was once a place known for its beauty, which boasted a handsome church, and a town hall where balls were held for the ladies and gentlemen of the town. For many years, Preston was known for its wool, linen and cotton industries.*
>
> *There's a sense of irony that Caleb was born in a place that provided comfort to others through its fabrics, and yet his own start to life denied him the fabric of what a child needs so much: protection and comfort from a primary caregiver. Childhood lacked a strong anchor, and this would impact him his whole life leaving him feeling as if he were lost at sea. With no one he could rely on for love and nurturing, Caleb had to learn to become independent, and his fiery nature often drowned in a search for self.*

From day to day, he alternated between feeling strong and weak. Exuberant in his risk taking, Caleb hoped good things were just around the corner.

With formative years which remained unstable, a strong sense of a loving family life eluded him. After the age of ten, he returned to live with his mother, two brothers and a sister.

It is a basic need of each human to have their life witnessed but how do we tell the story of a man for whom there are no willing storytellers? Well, this we know: his invisible storylines are with him forever more.

We can, however, look at the timeline of his long life through humanity's story during the past eighty six years that Caleb walked upon this Earth. For it remains a truth that he witnessed many stories in his life, and existed on this planet during times of great change. So many things that each of us takes for granted in our daily lives simply didn't exist and weren't invented when Caleb came into this world.

I wove in the following to link his life with a world event.

1967 will be remembered for the first successful heart transplant. It was also a time when there was a lot of heartbreak in Caleb's life, and proved life changing for all those involved.

Life brings us many lessons, but perhaps the one we're not adequately taught in school is that we can never really know another person's deepest anguish or highest hopes, and that unless we walk in their shoes we never fully know their story or the reasons they make certain choices.

Infant and Child Deaths

The death of an infant or young child, either preterm, stillborn, or with a short life (whether measured in minutes, days, weeks, months or a handful of years), is incredibly difficult to experience, witness and understand. It is probably the death most feared by celebrants when entering the world of funeral celebrancy.

The one question I hear over and over again from celebrants faced with writing their first infant funeral is "What do you write about? There's no life story..." I couldn't disagree more.

From the human perspective, we consider a long life to be a full life but we can live 'a lifetime' in even a minute or an hour. As with any eulogy, we're looking for detail, for meaning, for love.

Have you ever had the experience of walking along and then passing someone—someone you'll never see or meet again—making eye contact, smiling, and having that feeling live with you ongoingly? A lot can happen in a moment. A smile can last forever. Why was the person's smile so impactful? Because we FELT it. And when we write a eulogy, when we 'bring a person to life' for their ceremony, it is the *feeling* world we have to enter into.

As parents mourn the death of their baby at five months of pregnancy, they're grieving both the five months getting to know their baby: the kicks, the hiccups, the daily rhythm of when babe slept, moved, danced to dad's guitar playing or mum's lullabies in the bathtub each night; *and* they're mourning all the dreams that won't come to fruition: first tooth, first crawl, first laugh, first day at school, and so on. As they held their tiny infant in their hands, and kissed Lily's cheeks, then swaddled her, you can be sure there are stories. There are so many stories. Stolen moments. Feelings that will live in their hearts forever. These are the stories which will come to the page. This is your gift to those parents.

> *Lily always let Nessa know when she'd woken up for the day. There'd be a wriggle to the left, and constant movement until her next nap in the early afternoon. A favourite time of day was when her sister, Gemma, came for cuddles in the king-sized bed, and would talk to her.*
>
> *Gemma rubbed Nessa's belly with shea-butter oil, and together they'd talk to Lily about the adventures they were going to have each day: a walk to the post office, then a baby 'cino at Sally's Coffee Shop, followed by playtime at the park.*

At lunchtime, Raymond would pop home from work and strum his guitar while Nessa heated the soup or prepared sandwiches. Lily made it quite clear that she was a dancer. Crazy Little Thing Called Love was by far her favourite tune.

What Lily did not love, however, was garlic, crisps and vegemite sandwiches. For Nessa, it was worth giving up three of her chosen treats. After all, we do anything for those we love.

Bereaved Children

Some of the toughest funerals to officiate are those where a young child has been bereaved. I'm an advocate for children (certainly above toddler age) being at the funeral of a loved one. I've met far too many adults who were denied attending a loved-one's funeral when they were a child, and the lifelong impact that had.

My attitude is that if I can create a positive funeral experience, this will support their grief journey. The ages of the children I've worked with to create a ceremony have varied. In some cases, I've had them actively involved in a ritual or creating something. For others, I've read their handwritten tributes out, which is a bittersweet experience. In some situations, I've spoken directly to them during the eulogy, sharing examples of their time together. In a recent situation, the mother of the child decided he was too young (four) to attend his father's funeral. I wrote a section of the script as if I was talking to him directly. I then spoke as if he were in the room, and devoted that part of the eulogy to the father and son's relationship. Perhaps, sometime in the future, his family will share the script.

Suicide

Without question, the hardest ceremonies I've ever officiated were my best friend's cremation service, and then a few weeks later, her memorial service. It was torture to be in the role of celebrant and be a mourner. The services were about my friend; not me and my feelings.

Death by suicide carries with it many emotions. Guilt is common. When working with families, we ascertain the direction they wish to take the ceremony: do they want to raise awareness about mental-health issues or are they stuck in a place of shame and guilt and want no mention at all of cause of death? There's no right or wrong, and there should be no judgement. And regardless of the cause of death, as always, we remember the life that was lived (even if, like my friend's life, it was a difficult one).

There's absolutely no need to include the way they chose to die. In fact, at my friend's funeral (which her mother attended) I said she died from depression. At her memorial (attended by friends), I said she died from a broken heart. Both answers were true, and far more suitable than describing in graphic detail the reality of how her life ended.

> **Dolly's Baby Brother**
>
> Dolly Parton, the renowned Country Music singer, shared the story about how, as one of twelve children living in a one-room shack, her mother relied on the other older children to help with child-rearing. They were each assigned a child who was their special responsibility. The brother she was tasked with looking after, however, died at just four days old.
>
> I was really moved by this story, and the massive impact it had on her as a young girl, but also for the rest of her life.
>
> Research the above story, and then try writing about 'those four days'.

Regardless of what words you use, these don't need to form part of the eulogy. They can be spoken in the opening words or elsewhere, if at all.

Murder

When someone is deliberately killed, the shock and grief will override many of the warm and loving memories loved ones had. Our job is to gently find a way in and to go beyond the rupture in their hearts.

There's a delicate dance to be had, as with suicide, of honouring the pain, shock, trauma and tragedy of the death, and remembering a life.

Marcus had been well known in the community, if not by name then certainly by face. His job ensured that almost any adult will have come into contact with him at some point. And his smile, kindness, ability to be friendly with everyone, and his thoughtfulness is what he'll be remembered for. When he was stabbed, in a crime of passion, the shock reverberated around the small community. How do we write the eulogy of someone whose life ended so tragically? The answer is: don't define someone's life by a single day. There are places within the funeral ceremony, such as in the opening words, where I will acknowledge the shock or grief or untimeliness of someone's death, but for the most part, I keep the eulogy free of that. It's a personal preference, and of course I'm always guided by the family.

Sudden Deaths
If we could choose the way we'll die, most of us would opt to die gently in our sleep. That's certainly my choice. Few people end up with that luxury.

I'll never forget the day my younger sister, Ramona, phoned me from Australia. It was early in the morning, UK time. As she relayed the words that our father had been killed in a car accident, the scream which ripped through me was unlike any experience of my life. How was it possible? My father, superman, who'd survived a fire, pneumonia, malaria, a triple bypass, lymphatic cancer (twice) - and he's wiped out by a 17-year-old driver in torrential rain? I couldn't absorb the impossibility of it all. Dad was only 77. My father planned to live to 100! And he was in the middle of building a new home. No. No. No. It just seemed so unfair for someone who was a natural-born survivor. This was the man who, in his late teens, jumped ship from the German navy so he could emigrate to Australia.

Sudden deaths rob us of goodbye. There's a sense of feeling cheated. "If only I'd said that", "If I'd said this…" We can only hope, in sudden deaths, that our loved one died instantly.

Slow and Drawn-out Dying

Many mourners have watched their loved ones dying slowly over years, months or weeks. They've witnessed the person's suffering, weakness, pain, vulnerability and dependability. They may experience relief that the suffering is over, but with that comes a wave of endless guilt. Again, our job is to listen to their stories but to remember their loved one was more than their illness. This is such an important point. I have worked with many people who can't get out of the illness timeframe, and find it impossible to remember life before their loved one became sick. Sometimes, almost everything they tell me is from the time in the hospice, hospital or experience of hospice at home. As always, I listen patiently even though many of those memories won't be shared in the funeral. At some point, they'll find their way back to other times and share them with me.

Less-than-savoury Characters

We were all born in innocence. At birth, we were someone's infant, and we relied on them for love, nurturing, tenderness, affection and care. Some people have these biological needs met in abundance, and others are left wanting. And of course, how much of our life story is based on nature and how much on nurture? Whether you're a working celebrant or have never written a eulogy before, you may be called upon to share the life story of someone whose character could be best described as 'less than savoury'. Perhaps they'd been a wife beater, child molester or rapist, or their life had been marred by addictions to alcohol, gambling, drugs and so on. The first job we have is to be honest: *can we keep our biases out of the way?* If not, then the job is best passed to someone else.

I feel I can create a funeral for anyone, no matter how heinous their crimes (unless, of course, my own family or friends were directly impacted by their actions, then I feel it would be unfair to take on the role).

Why am I the right person to do such funerals? Because my own spiritual practice is one whereby I believe 'there but for the grace of God, go I'. I'd like to think my awareness and compassion would allow me to do the deceased justice, and offer healing to those left behind. I'm not the sort of celebrant who'd say "I wouldn't spit on their grave!" This doesn't make me a saint or holier than thou. It is simply a reflection of who I am as a person, and the path I've walked in life.

I certainly don't gloss over a person's negative traits or wrongful doings, yet I always come back to the meaning of the word eulogy: *true words (of praise)*.

A ceremony (of any description) is an opportunity for healing. It may be a time of relief, letting go of regrets, gratitude that someone who has caused harm is no longer in a position to do so. To be 100% clear, the job of an honest eulogy isn't to slander or judge someone: it is to *understand* them.

As a celebrant, I do believe one of my skills is having an awareness of human psychology: what drives us forward, what hinders us, what allows us to feel love, and so on. And again, I come back to the words of Joseph Campbell "Every story we tell is our own story."

The day we think we're superior to others, and stand in the position of judge and jury of someone's life story, is the day we should be honest enough to walk away from being a eulogist.

> *Holger's reputation goes before him. Indeed, you may feel as if you know everything there is to know about him and his life: many column inches have filled the press. Today, it is hoped that we may come to find peace, and lay him to rest. It is a time for holding your hurt and your healing, perhaps even in the same hand, and to acknowledge the interweaving of his story with yours, and how that changed you.*

No one is born with the name Holger the Horrible. This attribution by the press shows us a one-dimensional view of someone who could have walked one of many paths but instead took the one which satiated his appetite for hurting others. As he said himself, he lived with constant hurt that never left his side.

While it's common knowledge that Holger was an abattoir worker at (name) for several years, what isn't so well known was that from the age of four, when his puppy was hit by a speeding car, he'd dreamed of studying to be a veterinary surgeon. There isn't a single school teacher who can deny his exceptional intelligence. What happened? Where did it all go wrong? After all, as a teenager he volunteered at the local animal refuge and was highly praised for his caring and tenderness.

In his last year of secondary school, a fire ravaged their terraced cottage. Over the space of just a few hours, every last possession became cinder. Just days away from taking his exams, Holger's textbooks, study notes, and mock essays turned to ash.

The fireman said they were lucky to be alive. Holger didn't feel lucky. Due to the injuries sustained by his parents, neither of them could work. There was unlikely to be any return to normality for them. Despite the promising future which awaited him, Holger dropped out of school and applied for dozens of jobs. State benefits would never be enough to support the family.

We're not here to forgive or to condone, but we have an ethical responsibility to share the whole view of someone's life. Had it not been for that fire, and the cruel twist of fate, Holger could have been your local vet: the person you rely on when your cat, dog or tortoise needs saving. And this is the reality of any life lived: we hurtle along on this planet, our journey determined by circumstances and choice. Was Holger right to be so bitter? Was that fire and its consequences enough of a reason to go on and commit his crimes? Who are you or I to answer that? We weren't in his shoes, and we don't have his wiring.

In Another's Shoes

Choose one of the following people (whose background you can research) and write a few paragraphs of a eulogy for them. E.g. Rolf Harris, Jimmy Savile, Saddam Hussein.

Ending the Eulogy

The decision we make in how to end a eulogy is as important as how we begin one. It is vital that we don't just drop mourners off a cliff with an unsatisfactory or sudden ending. Here are some examples:

> *Andzelika enjoyed writing detailed lists of jobs to complete for the day, and was never one for procrastinating. Each and every day had purpose, and she found meaning in simple pleasures: the light of a candle, the scent of lavender, the way music touched her soul, the blossom of lily of the valley, the warmth of human interaction, and the tug of the tides.*

We are reminded of the pleasures in each day.

> *Derek lived his best life, and moved from day to day finding pleasures along the way. With a song in his heart, he got along with everyone, bringing joy wherever he went.*
>
> *Let us remember him, indeed, rocking all over the world and how much he thrived on holidays to Cuba, the Carribean, Dominican Republic, all over Europe and Canada.*

Derek had special needs, and his true joys included dancing and travelling.

Mei-Xing won't be having a headstone as this morning she was laid to rest in a beautiful woodland natural-burial ground. Given her immense love of nature, it is only fitting that she was buried there. Instead, in her memory, the family will place a park bench in the churchyard. This is such a beautiful way to honour her. After all, for 30 years Mei-Xing stood by the window of her office looking out across the serene churchyard. When it is in place, do go and sit upon the bench from time to time, and smile as you remember the part Mei-Xing played in your life, and how she will live on in your heart.

We have a sense of her past, and where she worked, and how her memory will be part of the future.

Life brought Deanna countless pleasures. Beyond her three much-loved children, she was endowed with six grandchildren, and six great grandchildren, all of whom she adored and "loved to pieces". Ever so proud of them, she was always interested in what was happening in their lives. Deanna left a piece of herself in the DNA of her descendants. Our ways in this world have been forever changed by Deanna.

~

If Narella were to look back across the years of her life, she'd say her main achievement was her children. In her life, she's known happiness

> *and heartache, love and grief, pride and passion, but through it all family and friendships have sustained her.*

The above two extracts highlight that family was at the heart of their lives.

> *With her poodle, Flossy, as a constant companion, Karina cherished her daily stroll along the shady paths of Coombs Wood in Armathwaite. To the soundtrack of the River Eden, they'd while away their time. Let us imagine Flossy and Karina there now, walking along the path. They turn around, knowing we're there, and Karina smiles at us. Then she waves, and continues on her way.*

This ending shows us one of the deceased's main pleasures in life. It also allows for a sense of goodbye.

> *Genevieve arrived into this world, on Pearl Harbour Day, surrounded by love; and she passed from this world, with her beloved husband, Richard, by her side, on a Winter's day, deeply loved, respected and valued.*

> *In the words of her friend, Wilma: "We shall miss her warmth, generosity, humour, steadfastness. Her love and understanding of the natural world. Her sharp intellect and her sensitivity."*

"What's The Time, Mr Wolf?"
You'll notice a couple of time signatures in the previous extract, as well as another literary element. What are they?

Full of spirit and joy, Loretta put her all into everything. Hers was a full and rich life suited to such a strong, determined, yet easy-going woman.

Always affectionate and tactile, and with a hug at the ready, she kept her door open as she waited for family and close friends. And there she'd be when they arrived: on the sofa and propped up with cushions; a huge welcoming smile on her face, and a feast in the oven or ready to take them out for a meal. Let us take comfort today that her years on this Earth were rich with adventure, dedicated to being of service, and filled with abiding love.

~

Lisbeth ensured her days were meaningful: whether it was breathing in the scent of a horse, galloping through a field with the wind in her hair, cuddling a dog, chatting with friends, improving her local community, or enjoying Jamie's love and companionship.

Despite her vulnerable start in life, or maybe even because of it, she finished this Earthly journey having loved and been loved. With her darling Jamie by her side, Lisbeth took her last breath and passed from this world.

~

Even with death in sight, Duncan was adamant that it was too soon to go. "There's still so much to learn, places to see, and things to do," he said.

In the comfort and familiarity of his home, with his loving children closely by his side, Duncan slipped away from this world knowing he was deeply loved.

~

Throughout her life, Priya has been sustained by the love and companionship of friends and family, her deep appreciation and knowledge of music, that dry sense of humour, quick wit, and propensity for fun, and her happiness in making a home here on the fellside.

We shall remember Priya, first and foremost, as a much-loved mama, friend, and as a protector of the people.
Elsa never said a bad word about anyone, and likewise, no one said a bad word about her.

> **I Spy**
> What literary techniques did you notice in the previous extracts?

Humour was her gift to this world, personally and professionally, and no matter where she went, Elsa made everyone smile.

The whole family gathered to be with her as she approached the doorway to leave this world: holding the space for her, as she made her transition. Elsa passed away surrounded by love. When we tell the stories of Elsa's life, we'll say "She made us laugh!"

~

Some people go through life strongly identified with a religion or other belief system. Tabitha would have said she was atheist. And yet, today, as we look across the pages of the story of her life, it is quite clear that she had a way of being and living in this world that was an exemplar of the highest version of humanity: She was kind.

Perhaps it's a quality that is easily overlooked in this fast-paced egocentric world, but for anyone who knew Tabitha Smith, that is how she will be remembered. Quite simply, she believed in being kind, and she proved this over and over again by her selfless actions to family, friends and strangers. Indeed, these acts of kindness were never things she needed to think about or debate; they happened naturally without a thought as to how it might possibly inconvenience her. On a moonlit night in November, Tabitha left this world with the same speed at which her mind worked.

~

We can measure Hannah's life in places lived, exams passed, relationships enjoyed with boyfriends and her marriage to Casey, or jobs she secured, and the countries she travelled. We can count her days through the pets, people and places she valued and cherished. What Hannah takes with her on this new journey is our love, and the priceless gift she has left for each of us is the love nestled in our hearts. Our beautiful Hannah left this world on a sunny Summer's morning.

~

Alizon loved to give the children in her class quizzes, such as: a guy sets out from his hotel and arrives at a crossroads but the signpost is on the ground. There's no Sun to guide him. Nor are there any trees. How does he find his way?

The above paragraph was in an earlier part of the eulogy with a pause after the question. The question is answered at the end of the eulogy in the next paragraph:

> *Quirky, a lover of words, humour, and curious about life, Alizon would want you to know that if you ever come to a crossroads, and the sign has fallen down, you'd pick it up and point it in the direction you've just come from.*

The next paragraph was for a woman who died by suicide, and wanted to raise awareness about mental health.

> *Many events in the past few years took their toll on what was already a lifetime of inner turmoil, and made it feel like the world was closing in around her. Ann consciously created her passing, and left this mortal coil, as she always called it, finally freeing herself from a pain not a single one of us can truly understand.*

Parting Is Such Sweet Sorrow
Reread the above extracts looking for writing techniques that you feel worked. The rigorous study of various examples will lead you to revisit your own writing. Also, consider the endings. Do you feel they worked? Why? If not, why not?

Remembering

One of the kindest things we can do for our loved ones is to write down the memories of our life so that when they organise our funeral, they have one less task to do. There are at least four or five ways to do this which immediately come to mind.

Notes
First person
Third person
Other points of view
Narrating with music

I'll look at each of these in a moment.

I find this is an excellent exercise for celebrants to engage in as well, as it makes them not only reflect on what is meaningful in their own life, but it helps them to have a wider perspective when writing other people's eulogies. What made our lives meaningful? How do we want to be remembered? Are we living the life of our dreams?

Notes
This option is as simple as referencing important or interesting moments and experiences of your life.

*I grew up on 700 acres of land in rural Australia.
*One of eight children.
*German parents. And so on.

First person

In this version, you write your life story as if you were speaking it directly. This can then be spoken at your funeral just as you've written it (and it will sound like you).

> *My early years were lived out beneath the expansive skies of the Darling Downs. The scent of eucalyptus and the Southern Hemisphere constellations were a constant source of nourishment. This is, no doubt, where my love of wide-open spaces was born.*

Third person

You can take what you've written in first person but flip it to third person. It might feel odd, at first, to do so but it makes it 'ready' for the celebrant, officiant or family member or friend who'll take the ceremony.

> *Amongst Veronika's favourite scents was eucalyptus, a powerful reminder of childhood: her days lived out beneath the expansive skies of the Darling Downs. At night, she'd sleep on the trampoline with her mother, but not before spending time studying the constellations and wishing upon falling stars. The trampoline kept them safe from snakes, and was a comfortable bed. Snuggled beneath duvets, mother and daughter would chat for some time. This deeply bonded and loving relationship remained throughout life.*

Other Points of View

A less common option, but perfectly valid, is to have a eulogy completely composed of other people's views and experiences.

For my fiftieth birthday, my daughters gave me the BEST GIFT EVER (most likely guided by their low university-student budgets!) They'd written to my friends and asked them to send a card or letter with a memory they had about me. They then glued all of these into a hard-cover book.

Oh my goodness, how I cried. I've had quite a challenging relationship with friendships over the years (because most of my friends live a long way away or I meet someone and one or other of us moves). I have a few local friends but mostly it is an area in my life where I have experienced 'lack' on a day-to-day basis. To have these beautiful recollections all in one book is priceless. I remember reading through it, then holding it close to my chest, breathing in deeply like I never wanted to let it go, and said "I'll have this for my eulogy. Just read all of these out."

I share a few extracts and examples here to illustrate how this might work to 'paint a picture' to an audience of mourners.

> *You are one of the few true honest and real friends I have met in my years on this Earth. You are a continual source of love and inspiration and nourishment for my soul; a Soul Sister, Care Taker, Hug Giver (Yes, I've*

felt every one of those supersonic hugs you send in my birthday cards), Ratatouille Maker, Lebkuchen Baker, Story Keeper, Star Reader, Wise Woman, Listening, Caring, Soul Baring, Heart-Sharing Goddess who I am blessed and honoured to call my friend. I love you. K

In the above, we learn that I give good hugs, take the time to send birthday cards, have certain foods that I'm skilled at making, that I write, am an astrologer, and care about those in my orbit.

We came to the village in March 2000. I remember regularly catching sight of you out and about in the lanes those first few years… enjoying the space and air with your two little girls trundling along beside you. It always made me smile to see you. You'd wave and have time for a chat, and I loved it when you would sometimes walk around the garden with me. Actually, when I think about it, there are many things I enjoy about you! Your hugs: lovely embraces that are always so welcome.

Your warmth. Not just your beautiful warm smile but also a warmth from deeper within. Similarly your gentleness. A deep and genuine gentleness that feels so comforting to be around. But strong, too. So strong. Always able to see a way forward.

But if I had to pick the one thing that I love most about our friendship it would be the honesty. We can talk through the most intimate of things and yet still both roll our eyes and laugh at the same time. We share many of the same loves and hurts. With love, D.

We learn that I like walking, spend time in nature, and we see the 'hugging' come through again. Through this friend's eyes, it shows character and personality.

And these two, from young children:

I rilly enjoy coming round to your house and reading fabulous books. I love all of your lovly incense that you have they smell gorgas. Do you remember when me, A and you painted your bench it was so fun. Oh how I love to spend time with you. K

I liked making popcorn with you in your kitchen. You're amazing at making things. I loved spending time with you. A

We get a sense of my home: it smells good (incense), there's nice food to be found there, and that creativity and books are important.

Our most favourite memory of you was years and years ago when both our families were going through exceptionally lean times. F was without work, and I was bemoaning to you about being so broke (as one does). At that time, we hardly knew you and Paul but what I will never, ever forget was your instant remark that

> *you had no money but had lots of food in your freezer that you wanted to share with us. How magical was that? Since then, our friendship has gone from strength to strength and I have even been elevated to the title of Aunty J. J & F*

This shows the audience: I'm resourceful and generous.

> *Dear V, That's how P referred to you in her journals:*
> *V is so positive.*
> *V is so strong.*
> *V has so much energy.*
> *I see that she was accurate in her observation of V. She had so much respect for you and loved your energy; and you exude it! What a year it's been. You've done so much good for so many people. A*

A is the cousin of my best friend who died by suicide the previous year, just days before my 49th birthday. From P's journal entries, there's direct insight into my nature.

As a child, three of my siblings couldn't say Veronika. I was called Hunda or Lala. My brother Rene still calls me Lala. Here is an extract from him:

> *It was quite funny having an older sister who was also my life coach. Lala was also so very keen to know about my current girlfriend and how things were tracking. It was always*

> *enjoyable when I had the Spanish inquisition into who, what, where, when and how on every relationship I was in (there were a few, I must say).*

Clearly, my curiosity gene was evident even then! (Tell me more, tell me more!)

> *The years of Lala being in England brought me many proud moments: The best was when I worked in New Zealand and a work mate's sister was talking about this wonderful alternative magazine on natural parenting that she'd found and was reading. I was chuffed. "Hey, that's my sister who owns and publishes this!"*

We learn that I published a magazine (The Mother magazine for 12 years) and how far reaching it was.

> *When I got to visit my sis, her hubby and my nieces in England was one of the most special times. To be spoilt with cooking and song and written word are memories that will stay forever. Seeing the love on Lala and Mr Lala's face made me see what unconditional love and kindness is all about.*

Above, we learn about my marriage and the joys which fill my day and that are then shared with others.

Below is from my first-born daughter:

> *The first memory isn't really mine; it's yours, but you've talked about it many times so it feels like a vivid memory for me also. It's about how, when I was a baby, you'd bake walnut and banana muffins while carrying me in the baby carrier. I always wished I could remember it myself as it sounds so peaceful, creative and happy. Also, those muffins must have smelled and tasted incredible! I now regularly make banana and raisin cookies for S and hope they're somewhere near as good as your muffins were.*
>
> *The next memory, I actually remember: It's every Christmas, and the weeks leading up to it. You loved the whole season so much, and I think that is actually an important part of why we did too. You were always so excited to put your Christmas CDs on, especially the Perry Como one! The Christmas dinners you cook are still one of my favourite meals, and I'm trying to replicate them for my family now. I really love, and always have, the way in which you incorporate German traditions into our Christmases. It's always been such an important and special part of it all: the stollen, the spiced red cabbage, and of course, celebrating on Christmas Eve.*
>
> *The other memory was only about a year ago. It was S's first laugh, and how happy you were to have been the one to make her laugh. B*

We have themes of cooking, home, mothering, grandmothering, love, ancestry and Christmas.

~

And now, to the man who has loved me for more than half my life. This is the person who knows all of me: the good, the bad, the ugly; and yet he's still here:

> *When we met, I couldn't imagine someone like you coming into my life, although you had apparently imagined me, so I guess you conjured me up! I loved (and still do) your vitality, your passion, your courage, your intelligence, your empathy, your use of apostrophes, and the way you looked (and look). I didn't seriously think that the attraction would be reciprocated. But life's like that, and it was rather like winning the lottery...*
>
> *... When we met, I had no idea of the breadth of your talents, and creativity. When they're matched with your determination, that's a potent combination: waterbirth pioneer, magazine founder and editor, author of fact and fiction, brilliant cook, my favourite celebrant, astrologer, my lover and best friend…mother of our lovely daughters.*
>
> *And underlying all this is your empathy. It's there in your written words but also in the actions of your daily life. You reach out to people who are suffering emotionally. I love the way that you don't just pay lip service to your feelings, you walk the talk. For instance,*

the bereaved clients that you've stayed in touch with, and whose lives you've enriched. You CARE. And I'm blessed to have the love you give me. I hope that we have many, many more years of rich life together. Your loving husband, P

From my younger daughter:

A few weeks ago, you told me you felt like you had no friends. And, given that I am Always Right™, I knew I had to prove you wrong. As you can see from this book, you are loved by so many people! I hope you can see that this book contains only a tiny fraction of the many lives you've impacted. So many people love you, and you have been such a huge catalyst for positive change in many people's lives ~ whether that be through The Mother magazine, your celebrant work, or through you recommending them magnesium out of the blue (You've definitely done it to randoms in Sainsbury's on multiple occasions!). I love you mate. E

We learn that I'll talk to anyone, wherever I am, and happily pass on knowledge or expertise if I think it might help.

And from this friend, a sense of my passion for natural health care, and there's the cooking theme again:

…whether it's been providing wisdom and balance, magnesium spray and arnica for

> *broken bones, or even baking a gorgeous vegan birthday cake (when my daughters forgot), you've not only said "I'm your friend, I'm here for you!", you've proved it. Thank you Veronika for your friendship. Your friend, E*

Hugs seem to be a recurring theme through these letters. Interestingly, during the pandemic when we weren't 'allowed to hug' I felt like I'd lost my currency. After each funeral, it was as if my arms had been cut off. I felt clueless as to how to comfort my chief mourners and their families.

> *Ever since I walked into the health-food shop in Penrith to see a photo of you on The Mother magazine I knew I needed you in my life. I was alone with my 14-month-old all day walking the drizzly lanes of Cumbria not knowing anyone. I asked C for the car, ran him to work first thing, the magazine on the back seat, in search of you!*
>
> *I drove around your village four times looking at each house. None of them were what I was looking for, address wise, so I decided "Heartlight Homeschool" would be friendly if I knocked and asked for directions. It was you!*
>
> *You opened the door and welcomed me in. And that was it, really. Ever since, you've opened your door and welcomed me in. I've valued your honesty and friendship. I love sharing your truth and your life. You're loving, warm,*

generous and funny. Thank you for opening the door, and keeping it open. I love spending time with you. Loads of love, S

So, if these extracts were shared at my funeral, I believe it gives an accurate picture of me even though it is through several different views. I share these here to show that it's okay to do things differently. It certainly doesn't make a funeral less meaningful. Quite the opposite, in fact. In every ceremony where I've been tasked with sharing a tribute someone has written, I have to work doubly hard to keep my emotions in check. Seeing who the deceased was through another's eyes, spoken in the first person, is so powerful.

Love Letters Straight From Your Heart

Think of five friends or family members (or even a colleague or neighbour), and write a page-long letter sharing your favourite memories or what you value about them. Feel free to pop these 'letters of love' in the post to them.

Consider writing in such a way that you're illustrating them in their life, and how you see them, and what their uniqueness brings to this world.

Narrating with Music

While it's not unusual to set a visual tribute of photos or video to music, another option is to have the deceased's favourite pieces of music played (or clips of them) throughout the ceremony as a way to tell their story. This is particularly effective for music lovers, or for people who perhaps are more private and don't want reams and reams written and spoken about their life.

This piece of music (name) was chosen by Frank because...

In this song, we are reminded of...

On Eloise's fifth birthday, this song...

This song, *Wide Open Spaces*, by The Chicks is the theme song of Veronika's life.

And so, instead of writing a eulogy as such, you weave narrative between each piece based on why the music was chosen, and what it meant in relation to their life story or personality.

The Hills Are Alive to the Sound of Music
Choose ten pieces of music to illustrate the story of your life with minimal narrative before and after each one. You might like to try this for someone else's life story too.

Editing the Eulogy

Quite possibly one of the most important parts of eulogy creation is in the editing. This is vital, not just to fit into any time restrictions at a crematorium, but for flow, structure and clear communication.

My own style is basically *write, write, write,* then come back and be more creative, and then edit ruthlessly. I find it hard to do final edits on the screen; so, from a printed version, which I read aloud, I search out the weeds which need pulling.

As I do so, I look for unnecessary words, over-used words, repetition, and so on. Editing goes far beyond checking for typos and poor grammar. Do I have enough action words to move my script along? Are there images to show the person living their life? Does that sentence make sense? Can I make that line feel softer? And so on.

This process should be a vigorous one.

Other Tips

The following tips are based on my professional practice as a celebrant.

I don't introduce myself in a ceremony before saying the name of the person whose funeral we're at. In fact, I don't introduce myself until after I've said *where* we are, and *who* for, and *why*.

I'll also welcome people watching via livestream, and talk about how it is an inclusive ceremony. Then, I introduce myself.

I keep myself, my thoughts and opinions, and so on, out of the script. That is, I don't say "I". Even when inviting someone to light a candle or read a poem, I don't say "I will now invite…" Instead, I'll say "Jack will now share…" The ceremony is not about me, my feelings, or my life. My job is to shine a light on my client/deceased.

Have you ever been to a ceremony where the celebrant/officiant/priest/vicar said "I didn't know Jack, but I hear he was…"?

I have never, and will never, say those words in a ceremony. As Petra Rigby, one of the celebrants we trained, so eloquently described the role: "My job is to reminisce on behalf of the family." Our role is to 'get to know' their loved one.

I recall meeting Eva, and in learning about her late husband, she also shared the story of the death of their only child, Carly. I asked various questions about Carly, and then wondered if there was anything about Carly's ceremony that she felt would also suit her husband's ceremony. Perhaps some nice touch? Eva said "The only thing I remember about Carly's ceremony was the celebrant saying 'I didn't know Carly' all the way through the funeral!"

Think about Eva's experience. How might the celebrant's words have been disconnecting for her? What purpose does it serve to say "I didn't know…"?

We
What I do in each ceremony is say "we". "We are gathered", for example. "We shall miss…" I'm comfortable saying "we", and being part of the collective, because I'm there as the family's voice. In the same way, when I speak the words of committal, I am speaking on behalf of them.

> *"Elysia Johnson, we lovingly, tenderly and with immense reverence offer your mortal, physical body to the embrace of Mother Earth."*

You All
Another thing I avoid in my ceremonies is saying "you all". Rather, I'll simply say "you". e.g. Warm wishes to you all on this Sunday afternoon compared to: Warm wishes to you on this Sunday afternoon.

> **Well, Howdy, Y'all!**
> Can you see why it might be more effective, more intimate and more engaging to drop the 'all'? It's a subtle thing, but what it does is makes it sound like you're talking to one person, or directly to someone, rather than an amorphous whole.
>
> Try writing a couple of sentences, one with 'you all' and one with 'you' and see how different it feels.

Acknowledgements
In many people's stories, there are acknowledgements to be said. It may be to neighbours, hospice workers, friends and so on. It's important to express gratitude, of course, however I find it works far better to include these in the announcements section rather than within the eulogy. Keep the eulogy focused on the deceased.

Many celebrants often either start their services with announcements or say them at the end of the ceremony. My preference is to include them just before the committal. Why? If announced at the start of the ceremony, unless an Order of Service has been printed with details of things like donations or where the funeral tea is being held, the mourner is likely to forget the details. I would never do it after the committal and curtains or interment as this is such a defining and gut-wrenching experience that to return to something as mundane as 'donations and tea' just feels, to me, wrong. I use the announcements section for thank yous, including thanking the funeral director and staff at the crematorium, donations, funeral tea, and anything else that's relevant.

Important Funerals

It is so easy to get caught into the idea that one person's funeral is more important than another's simply because they are more well known or famous. This does not make them more important than a person who has no mourners to witness their goodbye.

Some people, by nature or by work or other means, inevitably impact or touch many people's lives. That's been their life experience. As the person officiating the ceremony of someone with many mourners, we must keep our ego in check. Our dedication to creating a beautiful and meaningful service isn't dependent on the life which has been lived or the number of mourners in attendance.

Be mindful of not allowing your ego to think one person's funeral is more important than another's because they were famous, popular or well known in life.

Show the Script

Essential to my celebrant practice is showing the whole script to my client (not just the eulogy). Generally I aim to send through the script within 24 to 48 hours after my visit so that they have some time to see how the ceremony feels.

Depending on where you live in the world, you might have more or less time leading up to the funeral than I have. My ceremonies happen, on average, six to ten days after I receive a call from the funeral director. This isn't a lot of time to:
1. Arrange the family visit
2. Write the script
3. Organise the livestream, visual tribute, and music through Wesley or Obitus (in the UK)
4. Send through the Order of Service to a Funeral Director for printing
5. Have the ceremony approved by the client
6. Rehearse the ceremony.

Far too many celebrants don't send through their script. This isn't a practice I support at any level. The risk of error is too great. This might show up as an incorrect fact (in your note taking or their recollection). It could be that you just haven't hit the right tone or style.

There are many reasons why it is in your best interest (and theirs) to show your chief mourner the whole

ceremony script (not just the eulogy). Although I'm fortunate that my scripts rarely need any amendments, there are times when:
1. the client has incorrectly remembered something
2. they see their thoughts in print and realise they don't want Aunty J disapproving
3. forgot to mention something or someone
4. ...then change their mind and want names removed so other people don't get offended because they've not been mentioned.

Consider the showing of the script to be your best insurance. Also, if there are any amendments (whether additions, deletions or rewrites), resend the script for final approval and name each draft. For example: firstdraftjacksmith; fourthdraftjacksmith or finaldraftjacksmith.

I've heard far too many stories from unhappy mourners who endured a ceremony where it was littered with errors. And there have been celebrants taken to court for ruining someone's funeral because of factual errors. You are 100% protected from this if you show your script and receive an email reply approving your work.

I also include a cover page with the deceased's name, date of birth, date of death, time, day and date of the funeral, and location. If there's any discrepancy between what the funeral director told you, and what they told the client, this will be picked up. (Funeral directors, especially ones who take on too much work beyond their capacity, are prone to make mistakes. Don't get caught out!)

Of course, you can't please everyone in the audience. Your job is to meet the needs of the chief mourner. Ideally, though, you'll have more than one person giving you their recollections.

My overriding memory of my father's funeral? The celebrant pronouncing his name incorrectly all the way through the ceremony! My father had been killed in a shocking car accident. All eight of his grief-stricken children were at the mercy of a celebrant who hadn't bothered to learn to pronounce his name correctly.

If I ever have a name that is unusual, I write it phonetically, and I practise it until proficient. Please do the same. It might not matter to you, but it will to your client. The memories we leave with our clients stay with them for life.

Even if your only eulogy-writing experience is as a one-off favour for a friend or family, please ensure you show the script to them first.

From Writing to Officiating

If you're the one who'll be officiating the eulogy, the following tips will come in handy.

If you've written the eulogy, you have the distinct advantage of having written in your own style (unless you're only reading tributes from others). This means that your vocabulary and way of expressing yourself should shine through your words.

How do you get the words off the page? How do you breathe life into your stories? Your writing should be a good launching point. From there, rehearsing it over and over (I rehearse each ceremony about twenty times, on average), so that it fits like a second skin. My goal isn't to 'read' a script, but to have *meaningful eye contact*, *connection* and *heart-felt communication* with the audience.

One way I do this is to imagine that I'm sharing it, almost in conversation, as if I'm speaking down the phone to my best friend. There's a beautiful intimacy which comes from that kind of storytelling. It's a desire to really share information. When that fuels our creating, writing and officiating of a ceremony, people will remember it for years on end.

What Have You Learned?

If you've faithfully read through this book, and engaged in the suggested writing activities, your eulogy-writing skills will be enhanced. I'd go so far as to say that your whole writing practice will have transformed.

You've learned that: You don't have to write a person's life story in chronological order, and that our lives are not résumés.

Write That Eulogy has shown you the difference between a mediocre telling of a story and an illustrative one. This has been shown to you through many examples.

You've been guided in how to bring breadth, depth and meaning to the words you choose, and how this can illumine your writing. By now, you'll understand how to approach different types of eulogies.

With any practice, it takes time and devotion and discipline to build our skills. They don't just magically appear. After my celebrants-in-training have submitted their portfolios of various scripts, I always say: "Don't wait till your first paid booking to write more ceremonies. Start now. Talk to friends, family and colleagues. Ask your neighbour about their life. Every day is a writing day!"

If you're apprehensive about trying a new approach to eulogies with clients, start with your own eulogy. Consider all the things, people and experiences which made your life meaningful. Then explore writing eulogies for those within your family or friendship circle.

I hope you've enjoyed reading this book as much as I've enjoyed writing it, and sharing my experiences with you. Remember though, it's not enough to read it. If you wish to improve your eulogy writing, engage with the exercises, and consciously work on your craft. I promise you will see a difference in your style.

May the rest of your life be extraordinary.

We understand death for the first time
when he puts his hand upon one whom we love.
~ Madame De Stael

About the Cover Artist:
Sarah Louise Esau

Sarah is first and foremost a mother to two home-educated teens. She is married to Sean who she met in Coogee Bay in Australia, whilst they were both travelling many years ago. Sarah has over 20 years experience of working with young people both in mainstream and alternative settings. She's a passionate advocate for consent-based, self-directed education and has published many articles about education, the more recent ones you can find on her blog: www.unschoolsketchbook.com

Sarah loves to be outdoors walking with her dog, Legend, and observing the changing seasons. She has been a volunteer for mcsuk since 2016 and likes to import the wonder she experiences when immersed in nature into her drawings. She has always loved to draw and finds a deep sense of peace when sketching at home with a backdrop of music playing and a cat purring nearby. You can view her illustrations in her etsy shop: www.etsy.com/uk/shop/SLEsauArt

About the Author:
Veronika Sophia Robinson

Veronika has been guiding people through the liminal spaces of their lives since 1995, originally working as a wedding celebrant. Nowadays, she officiates across all rites of passage, with a particular affinity for eco-burials and crafting eulogies people will remember.

Although she eventually forgets the names of many of the people she's written funerals for, she *never* forgets their stories. There's always something to remind her of each person: the way he grew circles of orange marigolds in his front lawn, or how she saved up 20p coins for her granddaughter or how he trekked in the highland jungles or they volunteered in a remote Russian orphanage.

A late bloomer, Veronika completed her MA Creative Writing from the University of Cumbria at the age of 54 despite no previous academic qualification.

When not working as a celebrant, Veronika trains others, on a one-to-one basis, to be celebrants through Heart-led Ceremonies Celebrant Training, where she co-tutors with her husband Paul, a voice and presentation coach; and also teaches Masterclasses in crafting eulogies and love stories to celebrants around the world.

In her spare time Veronika writes novels in magical realism, and non-fiction books on a variety of topics.

A few of her favourite things: hot sunshine, hugs, steamy showers, Sun-ripened mangoes, tempestuous thunderstorms, travelling and exploring new places, reading books, dabbing jasmine oil on her wrist, singing in the car, spending time with loved ones, the sweet space of solitude, flowers - especially freesias, sunflowers, starflowers, jasmine and lilac; the rhythm of words, cloud-watching, laughing till her belly hurts, cuddling with cats and kittens, plant-based cooking, the sound of raindrops on a tin roof, her hands in the soil and sunshine on her shoulders, walking in nature, birdsong in the Springtime, and watching rom-coms.

Acknowledgements

My deeply rewarding path as a funeral celebrant began when Sylvia France entrusted me to officiate the ceremony of her beloved husband, Colin. Not only did his death, after more than fifty years of marriage, change Sylvia's life, it changed mine too. Thank you, Sylvia (and family), for your trust. And Colin, thank you for the honour of allowing me to share the story of your amazing life.

And to each and every grieving family who has shared their loved one's stories and memories with me, I thank you. It truly has been a privilege.

Although I've worked with fifteen funeral directors in my area, there are two in Cumbria who deserve special mention for their respect and consistent care with families, their professionalism, high ethics and kindness. Thank you to Tracy Lazonby of *Final Journey Funerals* and Graeme Kennedy of *Kennedy and Ferguson Funeral Directors*. You exemplify best practice even, and especially, in a (currently) unregulated industry.

Thank you to the celebrants who took the time to read through this book and offer their feedback. I appreciate you.

Special thanks to my darling husband, Paul, who is often neglected when I'm writing funeral ceremonies. Thank you for your love, patience and understanding; and double thanks for all those hot chocolates!

And to those whose deaths tore my heart apart, I still love you: my four pre-term babies; Bluey; Dad; and Pam. As Kahlil Gibran wrote "Your pain is the breaking of the shell that encloses your understanding."

www.ingramcontent.com/pod-product-compliance
Lightning Source LLC
Chambersburg PA
CBHW041927090426
42743CB00021B/3461